TACTICAL
CIVICS™

A New Way of Life
for Responsible Americans

Book One of the series

TACTICAL CIVICS™

Fourth Edition

DAVID M. ZUNIGA

Books by David M. Zuniga

This Bloodless Liberty

Fear The People (4ᵗʰ Ed.)

Our First Right Now

Tactical Civics (4ᵗʰ Ed.)

Tactical Civics Chapter Leaders' Handbook
(with Daniel D. New)

Coming in this series:

Book Two: Mission to America

Book Three: Engine of Change

Book Four: The Grand Imperative

Book Five: The Missing Peace

Book Six: The People Themselves

Book Seven: The Greatest Awakening

Dedication

For the responsible American of the unsung remnant,
who without recognition or pay and with few resources
today, faithfully performs the duty of every American
worthy of the name: preserve, protect, and defend
the Constitution for these United States
against its domestic enemies.

Contents

TACTICAL CIVICS™
Overview

In their 1998 book *The Sovereign Individual,* James Davidson and William Rees-Mogg described how the Internet would collapse governments and institutions. Now it's happening.

Millions prayed and voted in 2016 as God gave us an opportunity to repent and wake up to duty. Yet millions of Trump supporters still refuse to take responsibility as our enemy goes into full attack mode. America's long-festering culture war is now civil war. Nothing is out of bounds for the enemies of God.

The alliance to destroy America is huge: the corrupt Deep State, Hollywood, all major media, mega-corporations including Google, Facebook, Twitter, YouTube, Amazon, Target, Apple, Disney, Starbuck's and others – plus the NFL, the DNC machine and most of the RNC machine, teacher unions, the Clinton Mafia, the treasonous Obama junta and Soros interests.

This massive coalition shapes America's daily conversation while creating millions of negative social media messages to be used by fascists, communists, illegal aliens, Islamists and sexual deviants on city streets, campuses and online every day.

This is the first book in a 7-volume series designed to teach you how, with *only half of 1% of the American people,* we can restore America's rule of law and turn the tide of history.

You see, while the lives of humans – all 7.5 billion of us – are controlled by 1,500 billionaires and 7,000 other elites, we do not have to let them win, as you will see!

It's true that for centuries, the elite and their corporations and foundations have run the world using Deep State operatives. We seem to be another failed communist experiment like Russia, China, Europe, the UK and Latin America.

Mussolini defined *fascism* as the alliance of powerful central government with corporations to control the people. *This movie* exposes seven felonies in which Congress, presidents and the supreme Court have conspired for generations. They always make the first move, they use shrewder tactics, they own the media, and they plan ahead. Using puppets in government, the wealthy class plan their estates to assure that their descendants enjoy their lavish lifestyles, on your back.

But this is nothing new. As we explain in the free eBook *Fear the People*, America has been communist for a century. We're actually living in the most exciting time in history! For years, the Internet has been exposing the elites; now they're panicking. Their minions in the Deep State must now work harder than ever to distract us with political theater, foreign wars, and urban mobs.

I'm not suggesting that most Americans are awake; far from it. Politicians represent elites who own media, spouting propaganda from the GOP and Democrat machines and from Big Banking, Big Oil, Big War, Big Pharma, Big Tech, Big Insurance and others. Meanwhile, Americans send their children to gawk at 535 politicians who *each* spend $11 million annually on as many as eight offices. Their D.C. palace is as opulent as those of kings.

As they enjoy limousines, spas, and private jet charters and arrange for the top 1% of 1% to feed on productive America, D.C. recruits the Sodom Confederacy, Millennials, militant Islam, and illegal aliens to distract us. Then, instead of calling sin out, America's pastors hide in corners as the enemy destroys our civilization and public budgets.

But here's the good news: you can join the repentant remnant that is waking up as God is restoring tactical wisdom and common sense to our civilization. Followers of Christ know that it's time to start cleaning house. And we don't mean *talking* about draining the swamp; we mean real action.

This book opens a 7-volume series, an American's toolkit, if you will, to move beyond the problem to the *solution:* taking the responsibility our ancestors failed to take for the past 150 years.

The Deep State

DC organized crime is called the *Deep State* because we do not elect or even *see* millions of minions in unaccountable agencies, bureaus and programs nowhere authorized in the Constitution. Countless books have exposed the CIA and NSA as arrogant and criminal, keeping politicians and their sovereigns, the American People, in the dark supposedly for 'national security'.

While the Deep State regularly violates laws, its most effective weapon is government schools and colleges that erase history, civics, the Constitution and God from our national memory.

Tactical Civics™

The most accurate definition of patriotism is: *making our servant government obey the U.S. Constitution.*

Tactical Civics™ is the branded action plan of AmericaAgain!, with members from coast to coast. It has been developed by 40 volunteers including soldiers, sailors, marines, airmen, engineers, a former U.S. Secret Service agent, Fortune 500 tech manager, former naval medic and helicopter instructor, missionary, and others who have invested 10 years and 39,000 hours in the due diligence and R&D stage. Now we're launching county chapters.

Countless books, conferences, blogs, podcasts, radio shows and videos rehash the problem. They teach 'Constitution appreciation' but never *enforce* it. Why teach all about a law that you never intend to enforce?

TACTICAL CIVICS™ is We the People taking our proper role. Not social media chat, politics, or today's so-called 'militia', but a responsible new way of life: break Congress down into small districts, bring them home, enforce the law against them, and begin taking back all that we lost to criminals over generations.

Just Enforce the Law

As we explain in books 4 and 5, our mission seeks to restore constitutional Grand Jury and Militia duty by making them lawful, practical and cool. This is a new way of life with many aspects, and only one involves firearms. We intend to fight smart, move first, and reclaim the high ground. When We The People break Congress into small districts and bring them home, it will change *everything.*

As industry and corrupt public servants teamed up against the People, schools stopped teaching civics. Incidentally, the best definition of civics is simply, *who is boss.* To reclaim what we lost to D.C. organized crime, we need a servants-to-sovereigns role reversal that must begin with learning basic civics.

Mission Objectives

Step #1, a Proclamation Day event will be held at state capitols on a Saturday to be announced. See the new site OurFirstRight.org for details.

Then, TacticalCivics.com and AmericaAgain.net give you access to videos, podcasts, blog articles and eBooks to learn how we:

- Ratify the original First Right in our Bill of Rights
- Take Congress out of Washington D.C. forever
- Force through 18 other major reform laws over time

- Launch a new mobile app to enforce the Constitution together with restored Grand Jury and Militia in every county

Militia has been stigmatized for years. TACTICAL CIVICS™ is much more than just Militia; but making Militia duty relevant, cool and fun is part of the solution.

To start a county TACTICAL CIVICS™ chapter, join our national Facebook group here or MeWe group here.

Once you do the reading and understand the basic action plan, you are taking responsibility in your county. The next step is to recruit friends across America to start a county chapter, too. You can spread real hope by showing friends a full-spectrum solution.

The Deep State took six generations to control America, and we can't restore it overnight. But we can make history in our time for the sake of our children and grandchildren.

We Need Only Half of 1%

Throughout history most people have been apathetic; it's human nature. Margaret Meade said, *"Never doubt that a small group of thoughtful, committed citizens can change the world. Indeed, it is the only thing that ever has."*

This is not electoral politics; forget majorities. As we explain in Chapter 3, our mechanism needs less than half of 1% of the people to be involved. Elections can't do that!

Will Trump Support Tactical Civics™?

As with Reagan, heartland America crossed party lines to elect Donald Trump. He is not a cause but *effect* of a movement including Moral Majority, Christian Coalition, Constitution and Libertarian parties, Ron Paul Revolution, and the TEA Party.

Despite his opulent lifestyle, Trump claims to be our servant who must obey the Constitution. Now it's time for us to do the duties of our *higher* office, as Mr. Trump suggested in his inaugural:

"Today's ceremony...has very special meaning...today we are not merely transferring power from one administration to another or

5

✓ *from one party to another but ...from Washington DC and giving it back to you, the American People."*

Trump initially filled his cabinet with industry moguls, billionaires and family members; yet in under two years he has accomplished more than the previous six presidents combined. Our team has contacted his administration urging him to support our action plan:

✓ **2018-2020** we finish ratifying the 28th (original First) Amendment, shrinking congressional districts to 50,000 people;

✓ **2021-2022** we provide our Tactical Civics Good Guys slate of 19 reform laws to new statesmen running for the first 'big Congress';

✓ **January 2023** the first 'big' Congress enacts our Bring Congress Home Act. As his last official act of his second term, President Trump signs it into law, sending Congress out of D.C. forever;

✓ **January 2025** the ribbon-cutting for America's most historic redevelopment project: the U.S. Capitol building, now vacated by Congress and transformed into an historic museum-retail project.

We the People in America's 31,000 small towns and conservative suburbia elected Trump. Now we need to grow a nationwide network of chapters to keep this way of life growing.

On social issues, for 50 years a godless urban culture forced our civilization off the cliff, in our face, proclaiming atheism our future. Pantywaist pastors and authors cut and run, proclaiming 'post-Christian America'. It was all a lie; moral and ethical life continues in America's 31,000 small towns and rural areas.

The AmericaAgain! Indictment Engine™

We must stop letting Congress operate by 19th century procedures in secret, directed by industry. Chapter 5 introduces our proposed mobile app that will allow us to monitor our servants in Congress and state legislatures as easily as checking weather. Add in our restored Grand Jury (Chapter 6) and we can oversee indictment of criminal legislators, *from our mobile devices.*

Technology puts in your hand more information than the Library of Congress. With 78% of sub-Saharan Africa having cell service, an African herdsman can check the weather, learn English, and diagnose maladies that used to kill fellow villagers a decade ago. Given all the smartphone applications, it was only a matter of time before Americans created one to arrest D.C. organized crime.

Learn more about this fascinating mobile app now in the planning stages, in Book Three of this series, *Engine of Change.*

The ConCon Trojan Horse

Incidentally, the most dangerous George Soros project today is the 'Convention of States' scam. Read this article; especially watch the Robert Brown video debunking every lie peddled by con men, including the lie that this long list of liberal groups does not support the Trojan horse. Also note that politicians support it; another red flag.

Tactical Civics™ Principles

We don't need to replace our Constitution; we need to *enforce* it. Since basic civics is no longer offered in American schools or colleges, these facts may surprise you:

1) We the People, collectively (not individually) are *over* the Constitution. All three federal branches are *under* it. We're the top authority over all government in America.

2) Lincoln was a treacherous snake who hatched American communism. Read our blog article, *Lincoln: America's Hijacker* for six books on the subject. Sad but true.

3) By Wilson's era, eight of the ten Communist Manifesto planks were federal policy. By Carter's era, all ten planks were federal policy. America is technically *communist.*

4) The Supremacy Clause says that the Constitution, *not federal government*, is supreme; State judges are bound to *enforce* it as well as obey it.

5) The *Roe v Wade*, Obamacare, and *Obergefell v. Hodges* (pervert 'marriage') rulings could all have been avoided. In Article III, Section 2, Clause 2, we authorize Congress' total subject-matter jurisdiction over federal courts, to put certain subjects off limits.

7

6) Tactical Civics™ is law enforcement, not politics. You don't need majorities for law enforcement. With less than half of 1% of the population, We the People can do this.

This is the power that has always been ours! We The People are the only human authority *over* the Constitution. Voting is just one *minor* power that we enjoy by law; by ratifying the original first right in our Bill of Rights, bringing Congress home, and practicing Tactical Civics™, We the People will turn the tables on the Deep State.

Even if Trump is the best president ever, presidents don't run America; as we stipulate in the Constitution, *We the People do.*

So we get the public servants we deserve. Hillary would have been much worse, but let's stop treating a servant as if we're subjects and he's our king. As you consider the increasingly criminal operations of our servant government, the question is not how Trump will fix it. *He can't.* The question of our time is: when will *we* take responsibility?

Tactical Civics™ helps us come to our senses and return to duty. Even without President Trump's endorsement, *we* can end the hijacking. The following chapters explain how we will do it, and in Book Two, Mission to America, we explain this new way of life in a 7-week crash course. It's the civics we did not get in school.

To join a chapter, you must first be a dues-paying member of AmericaAgain! and membership dues is $5 per month; about the cost of a hamburger and fries.

Remember: responsibility is not for everyone, but to restore our republic we only need half of 1% to take responsibility. Don't worry if most people don't accept responsibility; picture in every crowd of 200 Americans just one person being willing to step forward. That's all we need.

You are reading this book because God gave you a sheepdog personality. Others may not care, but you do. Like me, you don't want to die of old age knowing that our government destroyed our lives and liberty on our watch. Tactical Civics™ is the only full-spectrum solution in the republic; a peaceful, practical, powerful new way of life.

So. Now you see this is *not* the end of America; in fact, it can be the best period in 200 years. God sent B. Hussein Obama and Hillary Clinton to make conservative America angry enough to finally stand up. Then He sent Donald Trump to show us what a gutsy non-politician can do against the Deep State. But ending the massive corruption in D.C. can never be accomplished by one man, for America is not a dictatorship or monarchy.

Enforcing the limits that we stipulate in the Constitution doesn't require a majority, either; only a small but dedicated remnant. For your county it can all begin with you; our *Tactical Civics™ Chapter Leaders' Handbook* provides step-by-step instructions on how to launch your county chapter.

Chapter 1

Ratify Our First Right

To take Congress out of Washington D.C., we first need a tactical preliminary to change the makeup of Congress – and by God's grace, the framers of the Constitution left us just the weapon we need: their original First Amendment.

The first Article in the original Bill of Rights, the only one that has not been fully ratified, has been gathering dust for over two centuries. Our first action project is to finish ratifying it.

The original First Amendment was designed to avoid exactly the corruption we have today: multimillion dollar campaigns with congressmen reigning over 750,000 citizens that they cannot know, much less represent.

Background

Two years before the Bill of Rights was finalized, on the last day of the 1787 Constitutional Convention, a motion was made to change one word in Article I, Section 2, Clause 4 of the new Constitution: "the number of Representatives shall not exceed one for every forty thousand" would read, "…for every *thirty* thousand". Others seconded the motion. George Washington rose to speak for the only time in the convention, as Madison describes on page 644 in *Records of the Federal Convention*:

"When the President rose...he said that although his situation had hitherto restrained him from offering his sentiments...he could not forbear expressing his wish that the alteration proposed might take place...The smallness of the proportion of Representatives had been considered by many members of the Convention an insufficient security for the rights and interests of the People.

"He acknowledged that it had always appeared to himself among the exceptionable parts of the plan...as late as the present moment was for admitting amendments, he thought this of so much consequence that would give much satisfaction to see it adopted."

The delegates unanimously voted for the change. For two years, State legislatures deliberated about ratifying the new Constitution.

In 1789, Madison's committee introduced 39 amendments and Congress finally passed twelve, called the Bill of Rights, sending them to the States to ratify. The Bill of Rights has 12 amendments but the first two, not ratified by the necessary three-fourths of the States, remained open in the States, gathering dust. *For two centuries.* Then in 1983, University of Texas student Greg Watson began getting 29 more State legislatures to ratify the original Second Amendment. After Watson toiled away for almost ten years, in May 1992 the U.S. Archivist certified that three-fourths of the States had ratified and that 'Article the Second' of the Bill of Rights was now the 27th Amendment to the U.S. Constitution.

Every article in our Bill of Rights is ratified except the first and most important one; it has 11 ratification votes and needs 38. So when we get 27 more State legislatures to ratify, the original 'Article the First' will become the 28th Amendment. If a mere college student could do it, so can we.

Congress Cannot Stop It

Since Congress already passed this amendment, Washington D.C. can't stop us, and no constitutional convention is needed. Our State legislatures have a *duty* to ratify our full Bill of Rights so we can finally restore the People's House.

12

What This Will Accomplish

Congress today spends $5.85 billion annually on operations, opulent lifestyles, their imperial palace, and massive staffs. No sane employer allows employees to set their own pay, staff, benefits, and office arrangements.

Making districts small will reduce House members' power; but our big payoff is that since Capitol Hill will not accommodate 6,400 House members and staffs, we can split Congress up and bring them home where we, not lobbyists, control them.

Chapter 2 explains the Bring Congress Home Act, stipulating that the 6,400 congressmen and 100 senators will now work full-time back home in one modest office each and be limited to two terms. We do not need a term-limits amendment either; remember, Congress limited the House to 435 seats without an amendment!

Proclamation Day at the Capitols

To announce this role-reversal, we will have a Proclamation Day event at all the state capitols except KY, MD, NH, NJ, NY, NC, PA, RI, SC, VA and VT.

Remember basic civics. Mob action is not for sovereigns, so we specifically do not want large mobs at these events. Even if Antifa shows up, this first action, Our First Right, is for *everyone*.

You order a 2-by-5 foot vinyl banner for the initial event on the steps of the capitol. We will send you the banner art to have the banner produced, along with the proclamation text. If you are a presenter, read clearly to the camera, assuring that your camera operator gets the entire banner held by two people on both sides a few steps below the reader so all will be visible.

If you think, *"A stupid proclamation? This isn't action!"* please keep reading. No 'save America' plan has ever worked because they have never offered a full-spectrum, lawful, peaceful, practical way of life like TACTICAL CIVICS™.

In this first public action, We the People demand that our servants in the State legislature do their duty under the Constitution. This is only Step One of the most powerful people's action in history, and this step we do not claim for TACTICAL CIVICS™; it will be an action for a coalition of groups from every part of the political spectrum. See the new website https://OurFirstRight.org for more details.

CAT Project

Appendix B is a 28th Amendment Fact Sheet and Appendix C is a model House/Senate Joint Resolution, giving your state legislators all they need to hold their ratification vote.

The next step is your state's Capitol Action Team (CAT), a group of 2-person teams who go to the capitol and get every member of your state legislature on video, answering one simple question: *"We sent you the Fact Sheet and model Joint Resolution calling for the ratification vote on the original first right in our Bill of Rights. What do you intend to do to pass this ratification vote?"*

To learn the history of the original first right in the Bill of Rights, read the free PDF pamphlet *Our First Right.*

14

Chapter 2

Bring Congress Home

Imagine being able to walk to your representative's office – or being able to run for the U.S. House yourself; just a normal citizen-statesman with no desire for a DC career. This was the founders' intention for "the People's House".

Our first AmericaAgain! reform law is the Bring Congress Home Act or 'BCHA'. Something like the 2013 resolution called HR287 proposed by Eric Swalwell (D-CA) and Steve Pearce (R-NM) to bring Congress home to work from their district offices via *telepresence*, which is common tech today, with thousands of participants able to meet by desktop, laptop, tablet or even smart phone.

The BCHA stipulates that all members of Congress will work full-time back home in one modest office each, with staff of two for a congressman or six for a senator; limited to two terms, and with congressmen making half their present salary since districts will be 1/14 as large. They will receive no benefits or pensions. Short-term public service, not a career.

What About Cost?

Even with 6,400 congressmen, with their small new staff and only one small office each, Congress' can operate just fine with their present $5.85 billion annual operations budget; see Appendix D. But that's just 15% of 1% of the entire federal budget of $3.9 *trillion* annually. We can radically cut federal spending when normal, productive Americans are serving in the U.S. House right from their own hometowns.

As soon as our membership is adequate to fund it, we will contract experts in telepresence tech, legislative procedure and fiscal analysis to perform BCHA analyses demonstrating the fiscal, legislative and security benefits of removing Congress from palatial facilities and updating its secretive 19th century procedures to 21st century accountability.

The Transition

Every member of our first 'big Congress' will first do what every member of Congress does now after winning office: set up the office and staff in their district. But then, instead of moving to D.C., they will simply meet at a large D.C. venue on January 3 (let's say 2023) for one task only: to enact the BCHA. Trump signs it and makes history, and every member of Congress returns home to their district. This historic reform is tailor-made for Donald Trump.

Besides the countless bureaucrats in the Deep State, there are more than 100,000 lobbyists in Washington D.C., plus that city-state is home to a vast network of predator-parasite businesses, consultants, suppliers and caterers. Massive, expensive government is big business in that city-state; it operates in precise antithesis to the rest of America, which only pays the bills. We the People can now end the hijacking.

Learn more about the BCHA at this link.

Chapter 3

Reverse the Regulatory Deep State

Even a fourth grader knows that We The People give authority to make federal laws only to Congress. Yet Congress only creates about 10% of all federal laws and regulations. Invisible, unaccountable, corrupt Deep State bureaucrats create the other 90%. It is time to end this criminal racket in which an ever-growing cancer of bossy paper-pushers, lawyers and clerks create and enlarge careers for themselves on our backs.

Our proposed reform law puts regular Americans in charge of 'sunsetting' all of the regulatory nonsense, over time and only after due deliberation. Most Americans just assume that because an army of lawyers and technical clerks write up tens of thousands of federal regulations, that we – the average honest business owner, tradesman, farmer, or homemaker – cannot review and weed out at least the few thousand most wasteful, ridiculous ones. If there is one thing the Internet is proving, it is that normal citizens can do amazing things when we work together to dig out waste, fraud and deceit.

It still needs improvement, but as of this writing the *Non-Enumerated Powers Sunset Act* is what you see on pages 58 to 65. Check it out; see what you think.

Like the Congressional Research Service, we propose that We The People need a Citizens' Volunteer Research Service of our own: honest, hard-working Americans serving on an ongoing government downsizing project, from now on...like serving on jury duty. We either do this now, or let our children suffer under the regulatory behemoth cancer already on every American home, business, farm and life.

In the following chapters, we begin to unpack our vision for the future, when that small but responsible remnant of Americans begins to oversee the law enforcement function of our state government and courts. Remember, most people will never take responsibility; it's human nature. Most Americans have become like Europeans and Russians and Mexicans…unlike their ancestors, they are now followers. But also remember that it will take only about half of 1% of the People; just one responsible citizen out of every 200!

Chapter 4 is only a brief introduction to the AmericaAgain! Indictment Engine™. For a more detailed explanation of how it will work and the profound impact it will have on our lives, read Book Three in this series, *Engine of Change*.

Chapter 4

Enforce the Constitution

Tactical Civics™ is predicated on laser-focus. We will only take on one project at a time, focusing all effort on that project until achieved. We will not fall for diversionary tactics including political theater and intrigue, vandalism, or street mobs designed to distract us.

Our ancestors did nothing for 150 years; we won't repair the ruins and arrest the criminals overnight. We will crawl before we walk and walk before we run. We have everything we need, but detoxing generations of propaganda still takes time.

Having said that, in this chapter we will jump ahead a little just to peek at an exciting key to our long-term objective: take back everything that DC organized crime has stolen from the American People over six generations.

Actual Organized Crime

Our servants have been perpetrating massive crimes for generations. In 1969, criminologist Donald Cressey published a book called *Theft of the Nation*. The international author, speaker, professor and consultant was the organized crime consultant to the President's Commission on Law Enforcement and Administration of Justice. The book exposed organized crime in all three branches of federal government, with taped testimony from criminal operatives.

Tom DiLorenzo's book *Organized Crime: The Unvarnished Truth About Government* exposes a century of Congressional crimes and disregard for law.

AmericaAgain! – The Movie describes Congress' top seven crimes: Counterfeiting, Fraud, Grand Theft, International and Domestic Racketeering, Extortion, and Soviet-style, criminal Invasion of Privacy.

So now let's be clear about the real battle for America…

TACTICAL CIVICS™ is not politics, an event, or a movement but a responsible way of life for those who decide to oversee law enforcement at the constitutional level.

AmericaAgain! is a perpetual charitable trust with a mission to educate, supply and tactically organize Americans using TACTICAL CIVICS™ to enforce the Constitution via the AmericaAgain! Indictment Engine™, a mobile app with algorithms that assign indictment target value to every bill when filed by a member of Congress or a state legislator.

Our staffing plan includes legal personnel to file the criminal presentments with each state Grand Jury and field attorneys and Grand Jury training materials to prepare and coordinate Tactical Civics™ members so they can inform and support grand juries and supervise state prosecutors, judges, and county sheriffs as we teach these servants to do their full duty for the first time in history.

Remember: in the Constitution, We the People give ourselves as Militia the power and duty to *"execute the Laws of the Union, suppress Insurrections, and repel Invasions"*. This is not politics, but a new level of law enforcement.

20

State Judges Trump federal

The Tenth Amendment stipulates that the sovereign States and People retain all powers except the 17 that we delegate to Washington DC, which *has no sovereignty in any other area of life or jurisdiction in any other area of the world.*

Read that again. Twice.

In the Supremacy Clause (Article VI, Section 2) We the People stipulate that *the Constitution,* not federal government, is supreme. We stipulate that State judges are bound by it. They are bound to *enforce* it as well as obey it!

Our Constitution has been massively violated for generations by our servants because We the People have never enforced it. From now on we will – in *State* criminal courts.

If you think a federal judge is king of the hill, read Article III, Section 1 of the Constitution. We the People create a U.S. supreme Court, then we authorize Congress (which we create in Article I) to give birth to its own *inferior* courts.

We did not create the State courts in the U.S. Constitution; our States were pre-existing, sovereign parties to that law. All inferior federal courts are created by, and serve at the pleasure of Congress; so in any criminal case involving a member of Congress, federal courts must recuse themselves.

As we explain in *AmericaAgain! – The Movie,* the U.S. supreme Court is complicit in Congress' longest-running financial crimes. And federal courts lack jurisdiction in State criminal cases anyway. So our legal authority is clear. As former Stanford Law School dean Larry Kramer suggests in *The People Themselves,* when federal government violates the Constitution, the People are superior to the supreme Court.

As U.S. supreme Court justice Antonin Scalia wrote in *U.S. v. Williams* (1992), a citizen on a Grand Jury is a higher authority in court than the judge, prosecutor, or sheriff. All this time we've only lacked a full-spectrum plan to lawfully, peacefully exercise our rightful power. *Now we have it.*

21

American Popular Sovereignty

The hierarchy of Legal Authority guaranteed by the U.S. Constitution

We the People

State Grand Juries   State Militias   State Courts

state legislators   federal legislators

state bureaucracy   federal bureaucracy   federal courts

How the App Will Operate

The AmericaAgain! Indictment Engine™ will let you see your servants' proposed legislation on your mobile device *before* it is passed, rather than having to lobby to nullify or overturn it *after* it wrecks your life or business. It will be scored for 'target value' – how badly it violates the Constitution and the sponsoring politicians' State Penal Code.

The Indictment Engine™ is a combination of a software app, AmericaAgain! Legal Section staff work, and peaceful, perpetual citizen action to superintend servants via *tactical force-massing*. Our Legal Section prepares criminal presentments beginning with financial crimes against residents of your State by a fellow resident of your State who happens to be a member of Congress or the State legislature.

The informed Grand Jury hands down indictments, then local constitutional Militia supports large numbers of citizens as plaintiffs in State criminal court cases against *individual* members of Congress for crimes under the politician's *State* laws that coincide with the politician's conspiracy to pass a law that violates our highest law.

Each time we get a State Grand Jury to hand down a criminal indictment against a legislator for a State Penal Code offense, with the full support of their well-regulated local Militia unit, our plea bargain deal will be like that offered by the Saxons to King Ethelred in 1014 A.D. or by the English barons to King John in the Magna Carta in 1215 A.D., or by Congress' IRS thugs to every Taxpayer… "Obey the law and agree to our plea-bargain terms, or go to prison with your assets seized."

Those members of Congress not yet targeted will receive the same offer, but as an immunity deal.

This is not rocket science. Public servants will stop colluding in felonies and will sponsor our reform laws restoring what D.C. organized crime stole from the American people.

Debunking Common Objections

Those who say that Congress enjoys sovereign immunity from prosecution are wrong. The U.S. supreme Court ruling in *Langford v. United States* reiterates a basic premise of 1,000 years of western law: no one is above the law.

Those who say that the perp will file for Removal Jurisdiction in federal court when indicted by the State court, are also wrong. Title 28 U.S. Code, Section 1441 is *only* available to defendants in *civil* cases; *only* arising under the Constitution or other federal laws; and *only* when there is 'diversity of citizenship' (plaintiffs or defendants from different states).

Neither the U.S. supreme Court nor the U.S. district courts have jurisdiction over a criminal defendant who is a resident of a state that indicts him for violating its State Penal Code, when all plaintiffs are also residents of that state.

Those who say that state prosecutors lack courage or honesty to indict members of Congress should be aware that in 2010, the State of Texas convicted Tom DeLay for financial crimes committed while he was the second highest ranking member of the U.S. House of Representatives.

AmericaAgain! Legal Section will brief and support honest State prosecutors and judges. For corrupt ones, the trained and briefed State Grand Jury can criminally indict the corrupt prosecutor or judge as a co-conspirator, and have their county's Militia back up the action.

Those who say that DeLay's was an insignificant case should review the State of Oklahoma's 15-count, $11 billion fraud indictment of WorldCom CEO Bernard Ebbers. He had his assets seized and is serving out the rest of his life in prison. The Oklahoma Attorney General allowed the federal court to take jurisdiction but was prepared to re-indict if the federal court failed to satisfy Oklahoma.

We the People can arrest organized crime that has considered itself untouchable. First we cut up the 435 huge, powerful fiefdoms into 6,400 small, local districts. Then we bring Congress home under our watchful eye and State criminal court jurisdiction alongside our State legislators. Finally, we keep legislators under full-time probation with the Indictment Engine™, the most powerful computer app of our generation. Restoring America is *entirely up to us.*

24

Chapter 5

Restore, Inform and Support Grand Jury

In pages 5-10 we explained all of the various steps in this new way of life. It is a long, tough, exciting challenge ahead. First, we finish ratification of the original first right in our Bill of Rights in 27 more state legislatures. That is explained in a free PDF pamphlet, *Our First Right*.

Last chapter introduced the Indictment Engine™ that will feed felony indictments to a State Grand Jury whenever a state or federal legislator introduces a bill that is found to amount to criminal conspiracy – which describes much of today's state and federal legislation.

Our Tactical Civics™ website and staff will educate, brief, and support your Grand Jury to play their pivotal role in keeping criminals at bay. For the sake of brevity, the remainder of this chapter is excerpts from Jason W. Hoyt's book, *Consent of the Governed* but without footnotes. For a more complete explanation of how we will restore the Grand Jury in every State, see Book Four of this series, *The Grand Imperative*.

We The People never gave our servant government the authority to create or control the grand jury. We never gave Congress the authority to pass laws governing how the grand jury must operate.

The fact that the Federal Rules of Criminal Procedure inserted a prosecutor into the process, who must approve and sign off on the grand jury's findings, is completely unconstitutional. As the *Virginia Journal of Social Policy and the Law* puts it,

"If grand jurors do not learn about grand juries from other sources, they will remain dependent on judges and prosecutors. Since neither is inclined to advise a grand jury of the full extent of its independence, the decline of the voice of the community will continue unless grand juries are provided an objective source of information."

Here are a few terms from the Fifth Amendment and their simple definitions based on historical and modern sources:

Grand Jury: *a group of peers who decide if a case before them should require formal charges.*

Capital Crime: *a crime for which the penalty can be death.*

Infamous Crime: *a crime involving fraud or dishonesty.*

Indictment: *a formal charge by a grand jury often brought forth by a prosecutor for approval of the grand jury.*

Presentment: *a charge that a grand jury brings by its own investigation or knowledge.*

The Fifth Amendment states, *"No person shall be held to answer for a capital or otherwise infamous crime, unless on a presentment or indictment of a Grand Jury."* I believe that presentment is the most powerful word in the Constitution. According to the *Creighton Law Review,*

"A presentment is a grand jury communication to the public concerning the grand jury's investigation...In early American common law, the presentment was a customary way for grand juries to accuse public employees or officials of misconduct. A presentment required no formal assent of any entity outside the grand jury. In early America, a presentment was thought to be an indictment without a prosecutor's signature and a mandate to a district attorney to initiate a prosecution."

We Have All the Power

Richard Younger's book *The People's Panel – The Grand Jury in the United States 1634 to 1942*, tells how America's settlers and founders brought the grand jury institution with them, implementing it as soon as they arrived, 150 years before declaring independence. They knew it had worked in England and that it would also be necessary to insure justice in this new land. The grand jury throughout history has been described as a "shield and a sword."

When the King wanted to charge locals with a crime, it was the grand jury, made up of peers — upstanding members of the community — acting as a shield that protected individuals from bogus charges. The grand jury also acted as a sword, investigating corruption by local officials.

This was possible mainly due to the *presentment* power to investigate on their own initiative; free from control by the very government they were investigating. They were, in essence, a fourth branch of government. The *Richmond Journal of Law and the Public Interest* states,

"One of the primary functions of grand juries in generations past was to investigate and uncover government corruption and misconduct. Upon identifying [it], grand jurors would issue presentments - published reports of findings."

True and immediate accountability occurs when a group of people, in the form of a grand jury, investigates criminal activity without waiting for or being controlled by a prosecutor or a judge. The grand jury is our fourth branch of government designed to hold the other branches accountable when they fail to do so themselves.

Before the *Federal Rules of Criminal Procedure* attempted to make independent grand juries extinct, grand juries were understood to have broad powers to operate even in direct opposition to judges and prosecutors.

In 1946, the Federal Rules of Criminal Procedure were adopted... The drafters of Rules 6 and 7...denied future generations of the traditional power of common law grand juries: power of unrestrained investigation and of independent declaration of findings. The committee that drafted the Federal Rules of Criminal Procedure provided for *only* a prosecutor-signed indictment.

U.S. v. Williams (1992) Majority Opinion

Now, compare this to the actual broad powers and independence of the People when serving as grand jurors, explained by the late U.S. supreme court justice Antonin Scalia writing for the majority in *U.S. v. Williams* (1992):

"Because the grand jury is an institution separate from the courts, over whose functioning the courts do not preside...

"Rooted in long centuries of Anglo American history, the grand jury is mentioned in the Bill of Rights, but not in the body of the Constitution. It has not been textually assigned, therefore, to any of the branches described in the first three Articles. It is a constitutional fixture in its own right.

"In fact the whole theory of its function is that it belongs to no branch of the institutional government, serving as a kind of buffer or referee between the government and the People.

"Although the grand jury normally operates, of course, in the courthouse and under judicial auspices, its institutional relationship with the judicial branch has traditionally been, so to speak, at arm's length. Judges' direct involvement in the functioning of the grand jury has generally been confined to the constitutive one of calling the grand jurors together and administering their oaths of office...

"The grand jury requires no authorization from its constituting court to initiate an investigation, nor does the prosecutor require leave of court to seek a grand jury

indictment ... [T]he grand jury generally operates without the interference of a presiding judge. It swears in its own witnesses, and deliberates in total secrecy. ...

"Recognizing this tradition of independence, we have said that the Fifth Amendment's constitutional guarantee presupposes an investigative body acting independently of either prosecuting attorney or judge.

"Given the grand jury's operational separateness from its constituting court... Over the years, we have received many requests to exercise supervision over the grand jury's evidence-taking process, but we have refused them all ... since that would run counter to the whole history of the grand jury institution, in which laymen conduct their inquiries unfettered by technical rules."

[End of Scalia quote.]

As the Creighton Law Review states, *"...beginning about 1910...the grand jury ceased to operate so independently... The practice of allowing a prosecutor to investigate crime allegations and then present his evidence for indictment before the grand jury became routine and evolved into such standard practice that by the end of the twentieth century it had become a part of "normal" grand jury operations.*

...Present federal grand jury practice, which forbids grand jurors from issuing presentments without consent of a federal prosecutor, is unconstitutional and violative of the historical principles on which the creation of the grand jury was premised."

Today's statutory puppet grand jury is not independent. They are controlled by prosecutors and district attorneys; not allowed to judge the law; not allowed to start an investigation on their own initiative; not accessible by the public directly; and the government picks who will serve on them. Members of today's grand jury are often *not* given full and accurate instructions as to their purpose and powers. Today's grand jury looks nothing like it did for over 700 years; it has been hijacked and severely weakened.

Few Americans have read the Constitution, know the limited role of servant government, or the massive authority of the People. Now you see why this new way of life is called TACTICAL CIVICS™. When you join a county chapter, you and your family learn civics; how to 'be the boss' over public servants when they violate our highest laws, and you learn how to avoid being manipulated by arrogant, lawless judges and prosecutors, too.

Many 'common law grand jury' members have learned the hard way: even when you know the truth, without a targeting mechanism for high-value presentments, and without the armed force of Militia deployed jointly with you, no Grand Jury can do its part to preserve, protect, and defend the U.S. Constitution and maintain America's rule of law.

Chapter 6

Restore Constitutional Militia

This is only a quick overview of how TACTICAL CIVICS™ plans to restore the true, constitutional Militia, and make it cool and fun for young and old. You can learn more on this subject in the Militia chapter of Book Two in this series, entitled *Mission to America*. For an even more thorough treatment of the American Militia and an accurate assessment of today's so-called 'militia' groups, read Book Five in this series, entitled *The Missing Peace*.

From colonization until Lincoln's war in 1861, America's defense force was the Citizen Militia. Under the influence of powerful individuals in industry and banking, Lincoln created a paid, full-time national army in direct violation of the U.S. Constitution, forcing constitutional Militia into extinction.

For at least five generations, We The People and our State legislatures have abdicated our duties. In its 146-year history, now with five million members, the NRA has done nothing to help. For several years, groups like Oath Keepers and III% United Patriots have built local and Facebook groups in most of the 50 states to gear up and train very sporadically, calling themselves 'unorganized militia'.

Dr. Edwin Vieira is the foremost authority on the history and constitutional law regarding the American Militia. His 2300-page eBook, The Sword and Sovereignty is the definitive work on this subject. He explains that there is no such thing, constitutionally, as *unorganized* militia. In fact, according to the Second Amendment that is a perfect contradiction in terms. Without officers appointed by the state (from among locals) and without the state providing for regular training, you cannot have a Militia as We The People stipulate in Article I, Section 8, Clause 15 of the Constitution.

Incidentally, that is the *only* clause in the U.S. Constitution where We The People stipulate a duty for *ourselves*.

Law Enforcement, Riot and Border Control

In that clause, we stipulate that We The People grant power to Congress to *"provide for calling forth the Militia to execute the Laws of the Union, suppress Insurrections, and repel Invasions"*. So when a citizen insurrection arises it is fellow citizens who are authorized to put it down, not a militarized police force or standing military.

Clause 16 stipulates that Congress shall have power *"...to provide for organizing, arming, and disciplining the Militia, and for governing such part of them as may be employed in the Service of the United States, reserving to the States respectively, the Appointment of the Officers, and the Authority of training the Militia according to the discipline prescribed by Congress."*

In other words, state legislatures have a legal duty to appoint officers and provide training and logistics.

Destigmatizing Militia

After decades of media propaganda, when most Americans hear the word *militia* they envision vigilantes or thugs. The Bundy family has made the stigma much worse. Most III% groups claim they are not Militia, and they are correct. In the Constitution we define Militia, as you read above. Playing soldier or Zombie Apocalypse in the woods – or prepping for disaster or economic collapse – may be necessary in case of an EMP attack or Great Depression II, but does not satisfy the clause 15 and 16 duties of constitutional Militia.

Our constitutional duty is to protect our communities from lawless government, insurrection, or attack by any power. From age 18 to 64, all of us can perform *some* Militia service.

Ending Urban War Zones

As former sheriff David Clarke said in *Cop Under Fire,* *"In a country with 325 million people, citizens can never abdicate responsibility for their own family's personal safety to anyone else – even the police."*

Clarke explains that citizens fear public servants due to a false narrative spun by Black anarchists, shameless politicians, and violent Hollywood programming that make 'peace officers' obsolete. Organized crime, gangs and drug dealers are well-armed; as Clarke explains, mainstream media lays down daily cover fire for these sociopaths. This relegates the Black urban community to life in a perpetual war zone.

Many gang-bangers were trained in the U.S. military at tax-payer expense. Increasingly militarized urban police forces resemble elite military but Clarke suggests that it's still not enough. Add in the federal alphabet agencies, open-ended 'war on terror' and Americans cowering in lines at airports and you see why 'unorganized militia' are forming.

Yet these patriotic Americans operate without the legitimacy or logistics (officer recruitment; training) that We The People stipulate in the Constitution, so the People and our servant legislatures are abdicating our duty.

Legislation to Restore Militia

TACTICAL CIVICS™ will work with governors to issue executive pronouncements to restore the appointment of officers and providing for Militia training once more. First, we need to have sufficient membership in the state to make a serious show of force at the state capitol as we make our demand, just as we need for the ratification vote on the original First Amendment.

We also need to push through our Militia Funding Act for your state. This bill will stipulate that anyone age 18-64 who cannot or will not serve in their Militia will instead pay an annual tax of $80 to support the Militia. Those funds go into a non-fungible (Militia-only) account at the state comptroller.

33

The funds will be directed to appointing paid officers and trainers in each county (about $50,000 annually per trainer) and reimbursing Militia members ($170/month) for gasoline and ammunition only when they show up for training.

Any 'militia' group could have taken these simple steps many years ago. Now we have no excuse. TACTICAL CIVICS™ county chapters will network with local retailers. Like the people of Switzerland, we will now become responsible for our own security.

Make it Cool and Fun and They Will Come

Militia duty is about much more than firearms, tactical gear, communications and training. Militia duty includes changing our view of who we are as Americans. With the first three words of our highest law, we declare ourselves the top level of government; the collective sovereign with *powers* and *duties,* not mere rights.

Like rural Volunteer Fire Departments, local Militia under State legislation needs to be an integral, valued part of the community in concert with other emergency responders and peace officers. This is responsibility like maintaining our homes and yards. The authority and duty to "execute the Laws of the Union" is ours, in concert with peace officers.

During the Roaring Twenties, golf in America zoomed in popularity; by 1932 there were over 1,100 golf courses affiliated to the USGA. We became the dominant country for golf and have held the position ever since. The pig-in-the-python was the PGA's huge PR push in the early 1980s. In 1980 there were 5,900 USGA courses; by 2013 the number of courses almost doubled to over 10,600.

Or take other armed activities: deer and turkey hunting produce food, but outdoor fun is the real attraction. Airsoft, NRA shooting competitions, boating, camping and kayaking all experienced huge growth with heavy marketing by retailers. Our plan is to have TACTICAL CIVICS™ help local retailers make Militia duty cool and as fun as other outdoor activities.

Tactical Civics™ - Militia Tools Beyond Militia

Today, with our rule of law violated by our public servants, our duty to "execute the Laws of the Union" is more critical than ever. The goal is to make service to your community an activity that you can enjoy with your buddies and older children. More than going to the range for an NRA competition, it must include muster and training in disaster relief, emergency preparedness – even urban tactical. As we stipulate in the Constitution, *"execute the Laws of the Union, suppress Insurrections, and repel Invasions"*.

But even more important at this point is law enforcement against corrupt and unconstitutional actors in government. Militia cannot operate in a vacuum; it must work with the Grand Jury as we explained in the last chapter. The Grand Jury must issue felony presentments against corrupt legislators, rather than today's unarmed 'common law grand jury' efforts against predominantly local corruption.

Article I Duty, Not Second Amendment Right

For weeks or months after every mass killing in America, the national debate heats up again, about our 'rights' under the

Second Amendment. This focus on this amendment is a dangerous diversion from the core constitutional stipulations concerning civil order and national defense. As you have read above, Militia duty includes law enforcement, riot and border control, and national defense. That duty and the power belongs only to constitutional Militia, not vigilantes.

We The People are arming ourselves as never before, but armed individuals are no guarantee that our republic and rule of law will be maintained. We The People, the sovereigns over this government, have never attempted to enforce the U.S. Constitution. Now we will.

National Firearms Act is Unconstitutional

The National Firearms Act of 1934 and later updates violate the Constitution and must be repealed. Given Article I and the Second Amendment, there is no constitutional limit on the type, caliber, fire-control system, optics or other features of arms that citizens can own.

It is unconstitutional for government to allow arms and tactical equipment manufacturers, distributors or vendors to tip the scales against constitutional Militia, saying 'sold to military and law enforcement only'. Any unit of our servant government becoming better-armed than the People is *precisely what Article I, Section 8, Clause 15 and the Second Amendment were designed to avoid.*

Besides enacting a Restoring Constitutional Militia Act in every state, we must repeal all state and federal laws that infringe on our constitutional duty (not 'right') to carry firearms whenever necessary for Militia duty.

Incidentally, open carry is *not* well-regulated Militia; it is a waste of time and only makes citizens even more fearful of arms – thus more suspicious of anyone even breathing the word, 'Militia'.

We must stop falling into liberals' traps, arguing about barrel length, magazine capacity, or open-carry, while every state legislature is openly violating the law by not providing officers and training for their Militia, and by infringing on the People's right to keep and bear arms for that purpose in every community. Yes...even in California and Connecticut.

The Monster We Were Warned About

Obviously this will not take place overnight; the cultural, economic, logistical, and other details of restoring Citizen Militia will take years to refine. It will also mean taking a hard, painful look at the massive military industry.

We fully support all active-duty and veteran citizens. In any case, today's military *defense* systems, equipment, aircraft, armor, etc will remain in place and always need to be kept up to date. But war is an industry like any other. The *offensive* aspect must be greatly reduced.

This means not only massive reduction in contracts for ruthless corporations labeled 'Military-Industrial Complex' by former 5-star General Dwight Eisenhower in his 1961 farewell address. It also means that this employer-of-last-resort for countless Johnnys, Jamals and Juanitos will need to cut back, and that aspect of the debate over military spending will be perhaps the most contentious of all.

Watch *AmericaAgain!- The Movie* and follow up with your own research online. We the People granted no authority for armed forces to project power for corporate 'U.S. interests abroad'. That organized crime complex has been copiously exposed in countless books beginning with General Smedley Butler's 1935 classic *War is a Racket,* and books by Peter Dale Scott, Stephen Kinzer, Andrew Bacevich, Douglas Valentine, William Engdahl, and many others.

When Lincoln turned DC's guns on his own people, our self-concept was transmogrified from collective sovereigns to cowering 'consumers' and 'voters', like livestock. America's Founding Fathers' gave many clear warnings against European-style military. If you are unfamiliar with the history of that war, or of the invasion of Hawaii and the fraudulent 'Spanish American War', research the books linked above. The war industry had its way for 125 years. That's enough.

Now, this hijacking by a subpopulation of military career families and huge war industry contractors, must stop.

As a civilization, we have fallen far from what we were. From a productive, missionary-minded people we began to cheer on a world superpower, 'deploying warriors' to plunder lands and resources of sovereign people. First this new 'world power' plundered these sovereign States. Then it began plundering far-flung sovereign people of the world. As the Roman Empire and the British, French and Spanish empires, we allowed ruthless men to own us for their own fortunes, causing us to be hated by half the world.

With statesmen like Sheriff Clarke opening a new generation of godly, practical discussion and with stalwart organizations like Oath Keepers and III% United Patriots doing such training and logistics as they can from their own pockets, there has never been a better opportunity to restore rule of law in urban America, reclaim 640 million acres of DC-occupied lands in the sovereign States, and more.

With over 70 million firearms owners in America, surely a few million can repent before God with Constitution in hand. With technology, wisdom and courage we can perform the duty that our ancestors abdicated. With principled veterans as trainers paid by their legislatures, we restore constitutional homeland security while re-employing veterans with valuable skills and experience to enforce our hijacked Constitution.

We can return to the ideals of honor and duty engendered in our Constitution – and make history as the world watches. Not primarily by using our arms, but by using our *brains*.

Chapter 7

Enact 19 Reform Laws

We will consider any candidate running for Congress to be a TACTICAL CIVICS™ Good Guy if (s)he publicly agrees to sponsor or co-sponsor the following reform legislation after taking office. The full-length draft synopses of the 19 reform laws are found in Appendix A, but we will give a shorter version of each reform law, below. In every law, there will be a clear statement that Congress recognizes the authority of every State Militia to enforce the provisions of that law within its State borders.

1) *The Bring Congress Home Act*, or 'BCHA' will bring Congress home, each member working from one modest office in his own hometown.

2) *The Constitutional Courts Act* will strip subject matter jurisdiction from the federal courts in all cases involving taking of human life from point of conception; education; sexual practices or the institution of marriage; healthcare and insurance; any foreign law-code proposed or attempted within any state; and any U.S. government claims of possession or jurisdiction over any land outside of that granted by We the People in Article I, Section 8, Clause 17 of the Constitution.

This law will make it a federal felony for any actor, agent, bureau, contractor or other representative of U.S. government to claim, own, maintain or operate a purported U.S. court or detention facility not located within the land stipulated in Article I, Section 8, Clause 17 of the U.S. Constitution, and all administrative 'law' tribunals will stop using the terms judge, court, order, subpoena, summons, warrant and 'the record', which are exclusively *judiciary branch* terms.

39

Finally, no federal judicial rules will have any bearing or authority over any State Grand Jury.

3) *The Non-Enumerated Powers Sunset Act* will instruct Congress to make available online, at no cost to the user, the 51 titles of the United States Code. The House will create the Standing Committee to Defund Non-Enumerated Powers (SCDNEP), to bind itself to obey the Constitution, and appropriate adequate funds for a website and support to serve a new Citizens' Volunteer Research Service (CVRS).

Each congressman will have (7) citizens from his district, called a CVRS Work Group, selected at random and overseen by an initial citizens' committee selected by lottery.

Prior to being funded or observed for a future fiscal year, every federal budget line item must be accompanied by a written demonstration that it falls within a specifically enumerated power in Article I Section 8 or Article II Section 2 of the U.S. Constitution or duly ratified Amendments. Every budget line item failing that test will be reviewed by the CVRS for de-funding and closure.

Any budget authorization appropriating "such sums as may be necessary", without specifying the amount, years, and specific constitutional purpose for which the appropriation was authorized, will receive no further funding.

Each Work Group's vote will be the vote of the U.S. congressman who represents that district; but no member of Congress shall influence, countermand, veto, or otherwise interfere with the final decisions of the CVRS, whether directly or through staff or any other agent.

4) *The Clean Bill Act*, will stipulate that no omnibus bills are allowed; that every bill passing out of committee shall treat only the subject found in the title of the bill, won't exceed 50 pages, single-sided, double-spaced, 12-point type; and that no committee can add any amendment, rider, or earmark authorizing anything not directly entailed in the subject and title of the bill.

5) **_The Secure Borders Act_** will fund the wall; will call for each border state to increase State Militia strength, and for federal airborne (drone) and ground sensor assets to be increased by 200%; will defund and discontinue each and every federal program, agency or office that encourages, facilitates, supports or defends illegal immigration. And Congress will assure that all individuals are barred from immigration who are reasonably believed to adhere to sharia law, regardless of whether the aspiring immigrant's domicile of origin is an officially Islamic state.

6) **_Senate Joint Resolution 6_** of the 111th Congress will end the illegal alien anchor baby practice.

7) **_The Congressional Anti-Corruption Act_** will stipulate that SEC insider trading rules shall apply to members of Congress; that no current or former member of Congress can lobby Congress on behalf of any domestic interest for five years after leaving Congress, or on behalf of any foreign interest, for life; and will make it a federal felony to require any member of Congress or their staff to raise money as a prerequisite to the member being considered for or offered a seat or leadership role on any committee.

8) **_The Citizens' Privacy Act_** will stipulate that the American people's persons, houses, papers, telephone, email, and other communications, vehicles and effects shall be free from any and all government surveillance, collection, seizure, storage, or detainment unless preceded by a bona fide judicial warrant issued on probable cause, per the Fourth Amendment.

It repeals every portion of the FISA, RFPA, USA Patriot Act, NDAA, and Intelligence Authorization Act of 2004 or any similar legislation presently in effect that violates the Fourth Amendment.

It places on Congress all responsibility and accountability to assure that all FBI, NSA, CIA, or other federal intelligence agencies scrupulously refrain from infringing on the due process of law, privacy, and freedom of speech and expression of every American citizen, and it makes it a federal felony for any federal actor or agency to engage in any optical, electronic, airborne, or satellite surveillance, collection, seizure, storage, detainment, tracing, or tracking of any American citizen, his property, or his communications, whether by means of traditional devices and methods or by 'nanobots', mini-drones, concealed cameras or sensors, or any other means, until a judicial warrant issues on probable cause.

9) *The Religious Treason Act* outlaws religious laws or seditious activities in the name of any foreign religion, state, or legal system operating within these United States.

It will be a federal offense for any elected or appointed U.S. federal public servant to travel to a foreign country funded by a foreign government or by a foreign or domestic private foundation or lobbying organization on behalf of any foreign country, people, or religion. Every lobbying group for any foreign country or religious cause, including Israel, will be required to register under the Foreign Agents Registration Act of 1938.

Every applicant for U.S. naturalization will have to swear under oath his or her full allegiance to these United States of America, their laws, and their security interests.

It will be a federal offense for any educational or religious institution, public or private, to promote or incite violence, war, or a foreign code of law on the basis of any religious teaching, tradition, law, or on any other basis than the security interests of these United States of America.

All individuals including American nationals, immigrants, resident aliens, and foreign diplomats, and all institutions within the U.S. who violate this law will receive a warning and fine for the first infraction, but further offenses will be subject to forfeiture of the individual's U.S. visa, indictment for treason or sedition, and seizure of assets held within these United States.

Upon the first instance of an individual or group associated with a foreign religious or legal system discharging a nuclear, chemical, or biological device capable of inflicting mass casualties, all U.S.-based properties, bank accounts, and other assets of that religious or legal system will be seized or where applicable, destroyed.

On the first instance of attempted murder by conventional explosive or mass attack (three or more victims) by any individual or group associated with, or on behalf of, a religious belief or legal system, using any potentially lethal object (firearm, knife or vehicle) there will be a nationwide warning of a ban on all gatherings in, or use of, any and all facilities affiliated with said religious belief system within these United States. On the second instance of such an attack, there will be a ban throughout these United States on all gatherings in, or use of, facilities affiliated with said religious system within these United States.

Finally, on the third instance in any of these United States of such an attack, all domestic assets owned by adherents in that religious and legal system within these United States will be seized and where applicable destroyed, and willful adherence to said system of belief or law within these United States shall thereafter be classified as sedition and treason.

10) *The Internet Liberty Act* will stipulate that it will be a federal felony to disable or censor the Internet so that it becomes inaccessible to the average computer or other Internet device in these sovereign States.

11) *The Constitutional Supremacy Act* will assure the sovereignty of the American People and States, stipulating that no provision of a treaty or agreement conflicting with the U.S. Constitution or not made in pursuance thereof, will be the supreme Law of the Land, or be of general force or effect.

No provision of a treaty or other international agreement can become effective as internal law in the United States until enacted through legislation in Congress acting within its constitutionally enumerated powers.

No Continuity of Government (COG) order may contravene, suspend or violate the U.S. Constitution in any particular.

Congress stipulates, as an Article III, Section 2, Clause 2 exception, that no federal court will have jurisdiction in any matter arising under this Act.

Any vote regarding advice and consent to ratification of a treaty shall be determined by yeas and nays and names of all persons voting for and against shall be entered in the Journal of the Senate.

This law makes it a felony for any individual or group to engage in or materially support actions that threaten the legal or financial sovereignty of any of the sovereign States of America without knowledge and consent of the legislature of each State whose citizens would be affected, regardless whether such action formally constitutes treason.

Within 12 months from passage of the Act, Congress must cease all foreign military aid and within 24 months from passage, all non-military foreign aid to any government, regime, entity, or individual. All foreign has to be immediately reduced by 33% for the first 12 months and 66% for the second 12 months.

12) *The American Sovereignty Restoration Act* of 2017 (HR193) of the 115th Congress, gets us out of the United Nations debacle, at last.

13) *The Lawful Wars Act* reiterates Congress' duty to declare wars, repeals the War Powers Resolution of 1973 and bars any administration from initiating foreign hostilities or mobilizing U.S. military in foreign lands without a Declaration of War. It requires Congress to assure that such mobilization or hostilities are necessary to defend against a demonstrable threat to these United States of America.

14) *The Federal Pork Sunset Act* stipulates that for three (3) fiscal years after passage, all revenues sent by federal government as grants to States must be remitted as a single block grant to each State with no federal conditions attached, and after the first day of the fourth year after the date of passage, any federal grant to a State or subdivision thereof will be a felony.

15) **The Minuteman Act** repeals the National Firearms Act of 1934, Omnibus Crime Control and Safe Streets Act of 1968, the Gun Control Act of 1968, the Firearm Owners Protection Act of 1986, and the Brady Handgun Violation Prevention Act of 1993; stipulates that no act of federal government or of any State or subdivision thereof, shall infringe on or burden the right of any citizen of any State who is eligible for membership in that State's Militia to purchase, own, possess, transport, manufacture, repair, alter, sell or trade any firearm, ammunition, or related accoutrements of Militia as that institution is recognized in the Constitution.

16) **The Non-Conscription Act** stipulates that government has no power to conscript Americans of any age into involuntary national service or servitude of any kind.

17) **The Return of Sovereign Lands Act** stipulates that the federal government has only the powers and authority specifically granted by the People and States in the U.S. Constitution, and that federal government has no lawful authority or claim of sovereignty over – or claim to minerals or other natural resources in, on or under – any land on earth, except as stipulated in Article I, Section 8, Clause 17 of the U.S. Constitution.

It stipulates that effective immediately, federal government cannot sell or dispose of any lands except such surface land as stipulated in Article I, Section 8, Clause 17 of the U.S. Constitution; that within 24 months of passage of the Act, federal government must relinquish all claims to or jurisdiction in, all land other than that which we specifically stipulate in Article I, Section 8, Clause 17 of the U.S. Constitution as its exclusive domain and 'possession'.

It bars federal government from seizing or even accepting private or State sovereign land, water, timber, oil, gas, minerals, or other natural resources in, on, or under such land in any State, for any reason, under any conditions.

It stipulates that all federally claimed, held, or controlled lands and any minerals, water, forests and timber, or any other resource within each sovereign State shall revert within 24 months to full control and ownership of the State in which it is located, to be managed and controlled as the People of that State determine.

It repeals within 12 months, all federal land-use regulations, national forest and park acts, and similar federal controls, restrictions, and prohibitions that deprive private owners of the full use and enjoyment of their private properties pursuant to the laws of the several States, shall be repealed within 12 months of passage of this Act.

As reparations for the past federal usurpation and plunder, it stipulates that all land, federal government improvements, fixtures, facilities, equipment, vehicles and other appurtenances located within each sovereign State (except on military installations) shall become the property of that State, effective immediately. Legal transfer of all said public property located within each State is to be administered by the government of that State, including executive, legislative and judicial branches and Citizen Militia as applicable.

Congress will provide to the sovereign People of the United States, within 12 months of passage of this Act, its detailed plan to relinquish control of all foreign military bases and to cease funding for, and operations of, all foreign land-based military and civil government operations, transferring foreign civil governance to the governments or people of those sovereign lands, within 36 months of the passage of this Act.

Including Puerto Rico, all noncontiguous, foreign, and/or 'U.S. possession' claims outside the 50 United States revert to the full control of the peoples of those sovereign lands at their own expense, with no additional expense borne by American citizens after 24 months from passage of the Act.

18) *The Lawful United States Money and Banking Act* will stipulate that only Congress has the power to coin money, and only to COIN money, and lacks the authority to refuse to perform this function; that the Legal Tender Act of 1862, the Federal Reserve Act of 1913, and all subsequent amendments

of those acts, have been unconstitutional since their enactment; that the special 'Legal Tender' counterfeiting concession given to the Federal Reserve cartel, has violated our supreme Law since 1916; that Congress will return in an orderly fashion to silver coins valued in 'dollars' at the prevailing exchange rate and gold floating with the market; that this new, lawful U.S. money is to be produced through immediate free coinage of whatever gold and silver may be brought to the United States mints, including sale of the existing national gold stocks, replaced by silver stock if the gold-silver ratio suggests silver as preferable for the initial coinage.

Said reserves and coinage and/or fully-convertible paper or electronic receipts for physical gold and silver, shall be substituted for Federal Reserve Notes as rapidly as maintaining a stable economy will permit, in all financial transactions of federal government.

It stipulates that the Federal Reserve system will have no official relationship to government, and that Federal Reserve regional banks must obtain new charters from the States consistent with the laws thereof or cease doing business as of the date on which the Secretary of the Treasury certifies that all financial transactions of federal government are being conducted solely in gold and silver or fully-convertible paper or electronic receipts for physical gold and silver.

The financial fraud known as fractional reserve banking is to be ended within 12 months of passage. After that, all American financial institutions must maintain in their vaults 100% reserves against loans made. If a financial institution accepting deposits is unable to repay on demand all such deposits in gold and/or silver or fully-convertible paper or electronic receipts for physical gold and silver, its directors, officers, shareholders, partners, trustees, or other owners and managers will be personally liable with their personal assets subject to seizure, to satisfy unpaid deposit balances under the laws of that State.

The law will make it a federal felony for any person to enact or enforce any tax or financial burden on: a) any exchange of one form of U.S. money for another form, or b) a citizen moving privately-owned money to or from the United States to or from any other domicile the citizen may desire, provided said funds are not being used in or resulting from illegal activity.

19) *The Intelligent Republic Act,* a reform law based very loosely on the Smart Nation Act sponsored by Congressman Rob Simmons (R-CT), must provide for orderly dismantling and defunding of all secret intelligence operations by federal government as recommended by former CIA officers Kevin Shipp and Robert David Steele.

The National Security Act of 1947 created the CIA and the National Security Council, which is accountable only to presidents. Congress, which represents the People and the States, allowed itself no oversight of the NSC. That criminal act of legislation never defined or limited what the CIA can or can't do and did not authorize covert operations that are closed to congressional oversight.

Even if the House Permanent Select Committee on Intelligence and the Senate Select Committee on Intelligence would try to de-fund the most egregious crimes of this criminal agency, the CIA makes it impossible. First, by making all of its budget line items and appropriations classified, secret from Congress, thus impossible to de-fund the agency in part.

Second, the CIA keeps blackmail dossiers on all members of Congress. No legislator would dare reduce that criminal organization's programs or funding. This is criminal blackmail, besides many other crimes against the People and our highest law. These unaccountable secret agencies must be dismantled, outlawed, and de-funded *in full.*

With illicit funding generated by foreign drug operations, these criminal agencies give U.S. presidents and even agency underlings, power over foreign governments.

Secret agencies unaccountable to the American people are unconstitutional and have increasingly destructive impact on American security, liberty, and public morale. It is clearly unconstitutional for federal government to create foreign operating agencies, fund private offshore contractors, or create alliances with foreign countries, whether for intelligence or supposed 'defense'. Such corrupt traditions violate the U.S. Constitution by usurping the authority of Congress and the Citizen Militia.

The Constitution stipulates that the Citizen Militia shall *"execute the Laws of the Union, suppress Insurrections, and repel Invasions"*. However uncomfortable this may be, it means that all networks, cells, and offices for intelligence in our republic must operate under their Citizen Militia and are ultimately the duty and authority of the People, accountable to the People.

Epilogue

Organized crime has filtered from Capitol Hill down to every city hall and school board meeting room. We seemingly have no control over this nightmare, like Europe or even Russia.

After 150 years of DC occupation of our States and our lives, TACTICAL CIVICS™ is We the People, finally taking responsibility. On this fascinating page of history, Europe is on its last legs against Islamic jihad and *failed Marxism*. Latin America is a train wreck after generations of corruption, drug cartels and *failed Marxism*. The Russian bear and Chinese dragon are both still reeling from *failed Marxism*.

And America is being twisted too, as you see: corruption, generations of adultery leading to serial divorce and cultural dissolution, 56 million Americans killed in aborturaries, communism openly touted in public – our original values are now drowning under layers of atheist, nihilist, transgender perversion in urban zones. And *failed Marxism*.

But here in America, we have a solution. After getting our own ducks in a row, we can put the fear of God into criminals, take Congress out of DC, restore our Founding Fathers' law enforcement, riot control and border defense, and begin passing our reform laws.

Yes, a lot of work to do. But do you have a better plan?

America is still the greatest country on earth. Our ancestors did their best but lacked the technology for an effective action plan. Now we have it, but until you become a dues-paying member of AmericaAgain! and help launch a TACTICAL CIVICS™ chapter, this new way of life is only an idea.

Now it's time to do the duty of every American.

Appendix A

The 19 Reform Laws

A candidate for Congress is considered a TACTICAL CIVICS™ Good Guy by publicly agreeing to sponsor or co-sponsor the following reform legislation after taking office.

1)The **Bring Congress Home Act**, or 'BCHA', stipulating: Whereas a general principle of constitutional law in these United States holds that no legislature can bind a subsequent one; and whereas the Apportionment Act of 1929 set a totally arbitrary 435-district limit to the U.S. House of Representatives in clear violation of the intention of Article I, Section 2, Clause 4 and also in clear contravention of the original first Article in the Bill of Rights as passed by the first Congress and sent to the States; and whereas a sufficient number of States have ratified that amendment and it has been recorded as the 28th Amendment to the U.S. Constitution; and whereas the expanded size of the U.S. House demanded by the U.S. Constitution, in light of the benefits and cost savings of modern technology and the security risk of Congress operating from one location, therefore:

Section 1. No member of Congress shall have a private office or staff located in Washington D.C..

Section 2. All members of Congress shall serve a maximum of two terms.

Section 3. No district of the U.S. House of Representatives shall contain more than 50,000 people, as stipulated in the original First Amendment passed by Congress in 1789 and recently ratified by the State legislatures as the 28th Amendment.

Section 4. To remain properly accountable and accessible to the sovereigns People that (s)he represents, every member of the U.S. House of Representatives shall be provided with a single office located within his/her district, paid staff not exceeding two persons, reasonable office expenses, and the hardware, software, and encryption technology and services required to conduct the business of the U.S. House of Representatives, working from his/her own district.

Section 5. To remain properly accountable and accessible to the sovereign States that the U.S. Senate was originally designed to represent, every member of the U.S. Senate shall be provided with a single office located within close proximity to the State capitol, also with paid staff not exceeding six persons, reasonable office expenses, and the hardware, software, and encryption technology and services required to conduct the business of the U.S. Senate, working from his/her own State capitol pursuant to such time as the 17th Amendment shall be repealed.

Section 6. Public funds used by any member of Congress shall be limited to the member's salary – which shall in the case of a congressman, effective immediately, be 50% of present salary; office staff, space rent and expenses; self-operated vehicle lease payment, fuel and insurance; coach-class airfare for public business; and mail costs to communicate with his/her sovereigns. An annual audit of expenditures for each member of Congress and his/her staff and office operations shall be posted online on that member's public web page accessible to the public, no later than 60 days after the close of each congressional session.

Section 7. Beyond those listed in Section 6 above, any and all other publicly-funded expenditures inuring to the benefit of a member of Congress shall hereafter be considered illegal use of public funds, including but not limited to: pensions and insurance premiums (retroactive), foreign travel under the guise of legislative business, limousines or other special conveyances, spas, hairdressers, and club memberships.

2) The ***Constitutional Courts Act***, stipulating:

Section 1. The American People stipulated in Article I, Section 8 of the U.S. Constitution, that "The Congress shall have power...to constitute tribunals inferior to the supreme Court...", and in Article III, Section 1, that the federal courts are, "such inferior courts as the Congress may from time to time ordain and establish", and in Article III, Section 2, Clause 2, that the U.S. supreme Court, "shall have appellate jurisdiction...with such Exceptions, and under such Regulations as the Congress shall make".

In 1799 in Turner v. Bank of North America (1799), Justice Chase wrote, "The notion has frequently been entertained, that the federal courts derive their judicial power immediately from the Constitution; but the political truth is, that the disposal of the judicial power...belongs to Congress. If Congress has given the power to this Court, we possess it, not otherwise: and if Congress has not given the power to us or to any other Court, it still remains at the legislative disposal."

In Ex parte Bollman (1807), Chief Justice John Marshall wrote, "Courts which are created by written law, and whose jurisdiction is defined by written law, cannot transcend that jurisdiction".

The power of Congress to create inferior federal courts, necessarily implies, as written in U.S. v. Hudson & Goodwin (1812), "the power to limit jurisdiction of those Courts to particular objects".

The U.S. supreme Court held unanimously in Sheldon v. Sill (1850) that because the People in the Constitution did not create inferior federal courts but authorized Congress to create them, that Congress by necessity had power to define and limit their jurisdiction and to withhold jurisdiction of any of the enumerated cases and controversies.

The high court even acknowledged Congress' power to re-examine particular classes of questions previously ruled on by the U.S. supreme Court, as stated in The Francis Wright (1882): "Actual jurisdiction under the [judicial] power is confined within such limits as Congress sees fit to prescribe...What those powers shall be, and to what extent they shall be exercised, are, and always have been, proper subjects of legislative control...Not only may whole classes of cases be kept out of the jurisdiction altogether, but particular classes of questions may be subjected to re-examination and review...".

In Lauf v. E.G. Shinner & Co (1938), the U.S. supreme Court declared, "There can be no question of the power of Congress thus to define and limit the jurisdiction of the inferior courts of the United States".

In Lockerty v. Phillips (1943), the U.S. supreme Court held that Congress has the power of, "withholding jurisdiction from them [federal courts] in the exact degrees and character which to Congress may seem proper for the public good".

Section 2. Therefore, Congress hereby excludes from federal court jurisdiction any and all cases involving:

a. Taking of human life, from point of conception;

b. Sexual practices or the institution of marriage;

c. Healthcare;

d. Education;

e. Any foreign law-code proposed or attempted within these United States or any of them; and

f. Claims of United States control, possession, or juris-diction over any land outside of that granted by We the People (the sovereign People and States) as stipulated in Article I, Section 8, Clause 17, U.S. Constitution.

Section 3. In Article III, Section 1 of the U.S. Constitution, the People stipulate, "the judicial Power of the United States shall be vested in one supreme Court, and in such inferior Courts as the Congress may from time to time ordain and establish"; therefore within 12 months of passage of this Act:

a. No 'administrative law' tribunal in these United States shall bind the citizen in any way;

b. No administrative adjudicator shall be referred to as 'judge';

c. No administrative tribunal shall be referred to, or refer to itself, as 'court'; and

d. No administrative process or tribunal shall describe its processes in terms such as 'order', 'subpoena', 'warrant', or 'the record', which are reserved for constitutional judiciary.

Section 4. Pursuant to provisions of Section 2(f) above and the proposed Return of Sovereign Lands Act, 24 months after enactment of this legislation and thereafter, it shall be a federal felony for any agency, agent, bureau, department, officer, contractor or other representative of the government of these United States of America to claim, own, maintain or operate a purported U.S. court or detention facility that is not located within the land or property stipulated in Article I, Section 8, Clause 17 of the U.S. Constitution.

Section 5. Because Rules 6 and 7 of the Federal Rules for Criminal Procedure have created a false, artificial barrier to the ancient prerogative power of the People when serving in their State Grand Jury, no federal judicial rules shall have any bearing or authority over any State Grand Jury. As U.S. Supreme Court Justice Antonin Scalia wrote in U.S. v. Williams (1992):

"(T)he Grand Jury is an institution separate from the courts, over whose functioning the courts do not preside...Rooted in long centuries of Anglo American history, the Grand Jury is mentioned in the Bill of Rights, but not in the body of the Constitution. It has not been textually assigned, therefore, to any of the branches described in the first three Articles. It is a

constitutional fixture in its own right...In fact, the whole theory of its function is that it belongs to no branch of the institutional government, serving as a kind of buffer or referee between the government and the People...The Grand Jury requires no authorization from its constituting court to initiate an investigation, nor does the prosecutor require leave of court to seek a Grand Jury indictment...[T]he Grand Jury generally operates without the interference of a presiding judge. It swears in its own witnesses, and deliberates in total secrecy."

Section 6. As stipulated in Article I, Section 8, Clause 15 of the U.S. Constitution, the several States retain the power to enforce this legislation by appropriate State legislation and duly authorized Citizen Militia enforcement action within their respective jurisdictions.

3) The ***Non-Enumerated Powers Sunset Act,*** stipulating:

Section 1. Congress hereby acknowledges as unconstitutional, any and all past enactment of legislation, 'positive law' Code sections and regulations, consent to treaties, or provision of federal funds applied to executive orders that confer on federal government any power not specifically enumerated in the U.S. Constitution or reasonably inferred from the powers enumerated, notwithstanding past creative interpretations applied by all three federal branches, to the terms 'interstate commerce', 'general welfare', and 'necessary and proper', and notwithstanding any and all positive law Code sections drafted, finalized, promulgated, and/or enforced by federal employees who have no direct oversight by, or accountability to, the American People.

No federal 'positive law' regulation shall create a legal duty or liability for any citizen of these United States, unless and until the agency purporting to enforce such a regulation shall have established beyond reasonable doubt that said regulation is clearly and unambiguously authorized by the People in a specific section of the U.S. Constitution.

Congress hereby acknowledges that the government of these United States is a constitutional republic form of government under the Common Law as opposed to the positive law traditions of many foreign countries, notwithstanding the massive Deep State that has created an overwhelming burden of federal regulations produced by bureaucratic careerists at staggering cost to taxpayers.

Congress hereby further acknowledges that ultimate sovereignty in our republic is inherent in the American People rather than in a bureaucracy that propagates, promulgates and defends thousands of new 'positive law' regulations annually, which are too numerous and intentionally too complex for the average American to grasp or understand, much less to oversee or diminish.

The United States Code is the Code of Laws of the United States of America (also referred to as United States Code, U.S. Code, or U.S.C.) and is a compilation and codification of all the general and so-called 'permanent' federal laws of the republic. But no law in this republic can be repugnant to the specific words and spirit of the U.S. Constitution. Any federal law which is found to be in clear violation of, or repugnant to the plain language of the U.S. Constitution is and has been null and void since its enactment.

The U.S. Code does not include regulations issued by executive branch agencies, published in the Code of Federal Regulations (C.F.R.). Proposed and recently adopted regulations are posted in the Federal Register.

Congress shall make available online, at no cost to the user, the 51 titles of the United States Code as maintained by the U.S. House of Representatives Office of the Law Revision Counsel, and the cumulative supplements which are published annually.

Section 2. The Standing Committee to Defund Non-Enumerated Powers (SCDNEP) is hereby created in the U.S.

House, to bind this body to obey the U.S. Constitution as actually written.

Section 3. Upon its formation, the SCDNEP shall appropriate adequate funding for a website and appurtenant support to serve and support the Citizens' Volunteer Research Service (CVRS) as described herein.

Section 4. In appropriating funds for CVRS website and support for citizen volunteers, Congress does not suggest that it, a federal servant, has authority to create such an oversight organ for the People themselves; only that Congress seeks hereby to provide for the People's oversight function to the extent that the People themselves require and employ it.

Section 5. Congress hereby acknowledges that the American People themselves, collectively, are sovereign in this and all other matters of federal government, as clearly and unambiguously stipulated in the Preamble, in Article I, Section 8 and especially in Amendment X of the U.S. Constitution, which sections only reiterate the People's original, God-given, organic, inherent, retained power to oversee all operations and budgets of their servants in federal government.

Congress hereby acknowledges that any CVRS Work Group or Supergroup casting its vote to de-fund and terminate any regulation issued by executive branch agencies shall infer that the CVRS has determined that the regulation in question does usurp, undermine, or countermand the stipulations of the U.S. Constitution or the retained powers of the sovereign People as stipulated in Amendment X of the U.S. Constitution. Said regulation shall become null and void and of no effect, immediately upon said vote.

Section 7. Prior to being funded or observed for any future fiscal year, any federal budget request whether executive or legislative – whether submitted by an agency, bureau, department, office, power, program, code or regulatory body, service branch, or via executive order or treaty – shall be accompanied by a written demonstration that it falls within a specifically enumerated power in Article I Section 8 or Article II Section 2 of the U.S. Constitution or duly ratified Amendment thereto, or can be reasonably inferred by the American citizen of average intelligence to be a rational appurtenance thereto. Any budget request not so accompanied, shall cease to be funded at the end of the then-current fiscal year.

Section 8. Because the functions of federal government were enumerated so as to limit the reach and power of the federal servant, such that it should never be considered either the master or the provider of the People, any agency, bureau, department, office, power, program, code or regulation not specifically enumerated in the U.S. Constitution or being an unambiguously 'necessary and proper' adjunct to the powers enumerated, as can be reasonably inferred by the American citizen of average intelligence, unless proposed and ratified as a constitutional amendment adhering to Article V of the U.S. Constitution, shall be subject to CVRS review and closure.

Section 9. In light of the long history of federal legislative, executive and judicial malfeasance and treachery by stretching the 'interstate commerce', 'general welfare', and 'necessary and proper' clauses, no federal agency, bureau, department, office, power, program, statute, code or regulation shall be added to others in any omnibus bill or amendment. If not enumerated in Article I, Section 8 and requiring application of public funds, each proposed agency, bureau, department, office, power, program, statute, code or regulation shall be proposed as a discrete bill or constitutional amendment.

Section 10. To maintain the delineation between the jurisdiction of an authorizing committee and the House Appropriations Committee, House Rule XXI creates a point of order against unauthorized appropriations in general appropriations bills. While any appropriation in such a bill is out of order unless the expenditure is authorized by existing law, if the point of order is not raised or is waived and the bill is enacted, said unauthorized appropriation is treated as legitimate. This practice has been tantamount to embezzlement of public funds.

Language requiring or permitting government action carries an implicit authorization for money to be appropriated for that purpose. The 'authorization of appropriations' provision limits the authorization of a piece of legislation to the amount and/or to the fiscal years stated. Accordingly, any prior budget authorization appropriating "such sums as may be necessary", without specifying the amount, years, and specifically constitutional purpose for which such appropriations were authorized, shall receive no further funding after the date of enactment hereof.

Section 11. There is hereby authorized a national Citizens' Volunteer Research Service (CVRS) with seven citizens per U.S. congressional district, comprising one CVRS Work Group, said citizens selected by each U.S. representative's staff at random from the legislator's congressional district tax and voter rolls.

No citizen selected at random to serve on a CVRS Work Group shall be compelled to serve. All CVRS members shall be volunteers, receiving no remuneration for their service to the public.

Section 12. As with a Grand Jury, all CVRS members selected shall remain anonymous, to protect the Members from lobbying pressure or threats, and from threats or retaliation by endangered government employees.

Section 13. The deliberations of each and every CVRS Work Group shall remain completely confidential within the Work Group. Divulging the name of a CVRS member or divulging in advance of publication on the 'More Constitutional Government' website, any decision of a Work Group to retain or de-fund a federal budget item – whether an agency, *bureau, project, code section, regulation or project – shall be a felony.*

Section 14. Each CVRS Work Group shall review individual federal codes, regulations and regulatory bodies and associated federal budget line items. Each CVRS Work Group shall review at one time only a single, discrete federal budget line item unless the powers and functions of the agencies, bureaus, programs, code sections or regulations entail several or many similar functions or areas of endeavor appearing to violate the U.S. Constitution, being neither explicitly nor implicitly authorized therein.

*Section 15. In such cases, an entire federal agency, bureau or regulatory entity shall be reviewed and voted on for defunding and closure by a **CVRS Supergroup**, which shall consist of twelve (12) CVRS Work Groups located in twelve (12) states, with two Work Groups from each region (Northeast, Southeast, Midwest, South Central, Southwest, Northwest).*

Such draconian action by 31 'mere' citizens (a majority of the 60 members of a Supergroup) compares favorably to the countless coercive actions impacting over 320 million citizens imposed by a single federal judge or at most by five justices of the U.S. supreme Court. As set out in the U.S. Constitution, the collective sovereignty of the American People is superior in authority to that of the People's servants, be they legislative, executive or judiciary, particularly when servants have violated the Constitution or occupy an office nowhere authorized by the People through that supreme Law.

Section 16. Each CVRS Work Group shall have 60 days to research, assess, and recommend de-funding and terminating a federal code section or regulation and/or its associated agency or office. At the conclusion of its deliberations, the CVRS Work Group shall submit the code section, regulation, agency, program or bureau selected for de-funding and termination, to the manager of the CVRS website, for posting.

Within 30 days after said posting, each recommended defunding and termination measure shall be voted on by each and every CVRS Work Group. Each Work Group shall cast one vote, representing the vote of a simple majority of that Work Group's members.

Section 17. Each Work Group's vote shall be the vote of the U.S. congressman who represents that district. No member of Congress shall influence, countermand, veto, or otherwise interfere with the final decisions of a CVRS Work Group or Supergroup.

No member of Congress shall recruit, entice, hire, contract, coerce or otherwise obtain the services of any staff member, agent or intermediary to influence or otherwise interfere with a final decision of any CVRS Work Group or Supergroup.

Section 18. De-funding and termination of any federal code section or regulation shall occur within 180 days of a vote having been cast with a simple majority of all votes cast, in favor of de-funding and termination.

Each such vote shall be posted on the dedicated secure CVRS website server for public access within 72 hours after the vote is cast, on the CVRS 'More Constitutional Government' portal.

Section 19. Pursuant to this legislation, the SCDNEP shall provide adequate funding and staffing to maintain a comprehensive database of each and every federal agency, bureau, code and regulation under review including date of commencement of review and effective date for de-funding and termination.

Section 20. No member of Congress or their staff shall interfere with any CVRS Work Group, other than each legislator's staff randomly selecting from voter registration or tax rolls, the citizens to serve on a CVRS Work Group.

Section 21. A CVRS member must serve a minimum of 90 days, and may serve on a Work Group for four consecutive years. No CVRS member shall serve for more than eight years in aggregate, with a minimum of two years intervening between periods of service.

Work Group members shall provide 30 days notice prior to resigning or retiring from service.

Every CVRS member rendered incapable of service due to death or disability shall be immediately replaced with the next name in the service queue in that congressional district and said replacement shall be summoned to begin service within 10 calendar days.

Section 22. No person shall serve on a CVRS Work Group if (s)he is presently employed by any agency of government or has been so employed within the preceding three years.

Section 23. Any current or former CVRS member receiving a financial benefit of more than $100 by virtue of his/her positive decision to retain a federal code section, regulation, agency, bureau, program or project shall be guilty of a federal felony.

4) The ***Clean Bill Act***, stipulating:

Section 1. No omnibus bill shall be permitted. All bills passing out of any committee in Congress shall treat only the subject found in the title of the bill, and shall not exceed 50 pages, single-sided, double-spaced, 12-point type.

Section 2. No committee shall add any amendment, rider, or earmark authorizing an agency, bureau, expenditure, office, power, program or regulation that is not directly entailed in the subject and title of the bill.

5) The ***Secure Borders Act***, stipulating:

Section 1. Each citizen of these United States has an inalienable right to defend his own life, liberty, and property.

Section 2. Attending that right is the duty stipulated in Article I, Section 8, Clause 15 of the U.S. Constitution, for Citizen

Militia to "execute the Laws of the Union, suppress Insurrections, and repel Invasions".

Section 3. Congress hereby acknowledges each border State's legislature's special right and duty stipulated in Article I, Section 8, Clause 16, to appoint the officers and train the Militia of that State.

Section 4. To aid in its duty per Clause 15, Congress shall provide for immediately constructing a secure border wall or fence, with reasonable alternatives employed for riverine sections of the U.S.-Mexico border, and Congress shall waive environmental, regulatory, and bureaucratic requirements such that the border fence project shall avoid the time and cost overruns common to federal government projects.

Section 5. Congress shall provide for an increase in border federal troop strength, airborne assets, and electronic detection as to furnish a demonstrably effective impediment to illegal crossing by any means.

Section 6. Congress shall coordinate this effort with the legislatures and their duly authorized Citizen Militia (where applicable) of the sovereign States of California, Arizona, New Mexico, and Texas, and shall accept all reasonable aid and alliance with said legislatures along their own sovereign borders, to timely construct said wall and/or fence.

Section 7. Congress shall immediately discontinue and de-fund all agencies, bureaus, policies and programs that encourage, facilitate, or support illegal immigration.

Section 8. As the Islamic belief system is well established and self-described as a militant organization and an exclusive, invasive law-code, Congress will assure that any individual shall be barred from immigration into this republic who is reasonably believed to adhere to sharia law, regardless of whether the aspiring immigrant's domicile of origin is an officially Islamic state.

Section 9. As stipulated in Article I, Section 8, Clause 15 of the U.S. Constitution, the several States retain the power to enforce this legislation by appropriate State legislation and duly authorized Citizen Militia enforcement within their respective jurisdictions.

6) ***Senate Joint Resolution 6*** of the 111th Congress, ending the illegal aliens' anchor baby practice.

7) The ***Congressional Anti-Corruption Act***, stipulating:

Section 1. SEC insider trading rules shall apply to members of Congress. It shall be a federal crime for a member of Congress, directly or through proxies, trusts, or other entities, to purchase or sell stock in any company materially affected by legislation of which the member of Congress may be reasonably expected to have knowledge.

Section 2. No incumbent or former member of Congress may lobby Congress on behalf of any domestic interest for a period of five years after leaving Congress, or on behalf of any foreign interest, for life.

Section 3. For any member of Congress to require any member to raise money as a prerequisite to being considered for or offered a seat or leadership role on any committee of Congress, shall be a federal felony.

Section 4. As stipulated in Article I, Section 8, Clause 15 of the U.S. Constitution, the several States retain the power to enforce this legislation by appropriate State legislation and duly authorized Citizen Militia enforcement within their respective jurisdictions.

8) The ***Citizens' Privacy Act***, stipulating:

Section 1. The American people's own persons, houses, papers, telephone, email, and other communications, vehicles and effects shall be free from any and all government surveillance, collection, seizure, storage, or detainment unless preceded by issuance of a specific, bona fide judicial warrant issued upon probable cause, as stipulated in the Fourth Amendment to the U.S. Constitution.

Section 2. With the benefit of the doubt accruing to the citizen, any portion of the FISA, RFPA, USA Patriot Act, NDAA, and Intelligence Authorization Act of 2004 or any similar legislation presently in effect that violates the Fourth Amendment, are hereby repealed.

Section 3. Congress shall bear responsibility and accountability to the American People to assure that any operations of the FBI, NSA, CIA, or any other federal intelligence agency shall scrupulously refrain from infringing on the due process of law, privacy, and freedom of speech and expression of any American citizen, whether residing in any of the 50 sovereign States or residing temporarily overseas.

Section 4. It shall be a federal felony for any individual or federal entity to engage in any optical, electronic, airborne, or satellite surveillance, collection, seizure, storage, detainment, tracing, or tracking of any American citizen, his property, or his communications, whether by means of traditional devices and methods or by 'nanobots', mini-drones, concealed cameras or sensors, or any other means, until a judicial warrant is issued upon probable cause, supported by oath or affirmation and particularly describing place, items, or data to be searched and persons or things to be seized.

Section 5. No visa of an American citizen seeking to return to one of the 50 sovereign States, shall be revoked without due process of law.

Section 6. As stipulated in Article I, Section 8, Clause 15 of the U.S. Constitution, the several States retain the power to enforce this legislation by appropriate State legislation and duly authorized Citizen Militia enforcement within their respective jurisdictions.

9) The ***Religious Treason Act,*** outlawing religious laws or seditious activities in the name of any foreign religion, state, or legal system operating within these United States, stipulating as follows:

Section 1. It shall be a federal offense for any elected or appointed U.S. federal public servant to travel to a foreign country with such travel funded by a foreign government or by a foreign or domestic private foundation or lobbying organization on behalf of any foreign country, people, or religion.

Section 2. Every lobbying group for any foreign country or religious cause – specifically any lobbying organization for Israel or any Islamic state – is required to register within 180 days of passage of this legislation, under the Foreign Agents Registration Act of 1938.

Section 3. Every applicant for U.S. naturalization shall be required to swear under oath his or her full allegiance to these United States of America, their laws, and their security interests.

Section 4. It shall be a federal offense for any educational or religious institution, public or private, to promote or incite violence, war, or a foreign code of law on the basis of any religious teaching, tradition, law, or on any other basis than the security interests of these United States of America.

Section 5. All individuals including American nationals, immigrants, resident aliens, and foreign diplomats, and all institutions within these United States found in violation of this law shall receive a warning and fine for the first infraction. Further offense(s) shall be subject to forfeiture of the individual's U.S. visa, indictment for treason or sedition, and seizure of assets held within these United States.

Section 6. Upon the first instance of an individual or group associated with a foreign religious or legal system, discharging in any of these United States a nuclear, chemical, or biological device capable of inflicting mass casual-ties: all U.S.-based land, buildings, training facilities, bank accounts, and other assets of said religious or legal system shall be seized and where applicable, destroyed.

Section 7. Upon the first instance in any of these United States of attempted murder by conventional explosive or mass attack (three or more victims) by any individual or group associated with, or on behalf of, a religious belief or legal system, using any potentially lethal object (firearm, knife or vehicle) there shall issue a nationwide warning of a ban on all gatherings in, or use of, any and all facilities affiliated with said religious belief system within these United States.

Section 8. Upon the second instance in any of these United States of attempted murder by conventional explosive or mass attack (three or more victims) by any individual or group associated with, or on behalf of, a religious belief or legal system, using any potentially lethal object (firearm, knife or vehicle) there shall issue a ban throughout these United States on all gatherings in, or use of, any and all facilities affiliated with said religious system within these United States.

Section 9. Upon the third instance in any of these United States of attempted murder by conventional explosive or mass attack (three or more victims) by any individual or group associated with, or on behalf of, a religious belief or legal system, using any potentially lethal object (firearm, knife or vehicle), all property and other assets held by or in favor of, said religious system within these United States shall be seized and where applicable destroyed, and willful adherence to said system of belief or law within these United States shall thereafter be classified as sedition and treason.

Section 10. As stipulated in Article I, Section 8, Clause 15 of the U.S. Constitution, the several States retain the power to enforce this legislation by appropriate State legislation and duly authorized Citizen Militia enforcement within their respective jurisdictions.

10) The ***Internet Liberty Act***, stipulating:

Section 1. It shall be a federal felony for any individual or group within federal government who – unilaterally or with other individuals, groups, organizations, or foreign governments – disables or censors the Internet so that it becomes inaccessible to the average computer or other Internet device in these sovereign States.

Section 2. As stipulated in Article I, Section 8, Clause 15 of the U.S. Constitution, the several States retain the power to enforce this legislation by appropriate State legislation and duly authorized Citizen Militia enforcement within their respective jurisdictions.

11) The ***Constitutional Supremacy Act***, assuring the sovereignty of the American People and States, stipulating:

Section 1. No provision of a treaty or agreement, public or secret, conflicting with this Constitution or not made in pursuance thereof, shall be the supreme Law of the Land or be of general force or effect.

Section 2. No provision of a treaty or other international agreement shall become effective as internal law in the United States until it is enacted through legislation in Congress acting within its constitutionally enumerated powers.

Section 3. No Continuity of Government (COG) order may contravene, suspend or violate the U.S. Constitution in any particular.

Section 4. Per Article III, Section 2, Clause 2 of the U.S. Constitution, Congress hereby stipulates as an Exception that no federal court shall have jurisdiction in any matter arising under this Act.

Section 5. Any vote regarding advice and consent to ratification of a treaty shall be determined by yeas and nays and names of all persons voting for and against shall be entered in the Journal of the Senate.

Section 6. It shall be a federal felony for any individual or group to engage in or to materially support actions that threaten the legal or financial sovereignty of any of the sovereign States of America without the knowledge and consent of the legislature of each and every State whose citizens would be affected, regardless whether such action may formally constitute treason.

Section 7. Within 12 months from passage of this Act, Congress shall cease all foreign aid of a military nature to any government, regime, entity, or individual.

Section 8. Within 24 months from passage of this Act, Congress shall cease all foreign aid of a non-military nature to any government, regime, entity, or individual. Said aid shall be immediately reduced by 33% for the first 12 months and by 66% for the second 12 months.

12) The ***American Sovereignty Restoration Act*** of 2017 (HR193) of the 115th Congress, and stipulating:

Section 1. This bill repeals the United Nations Participation Act of 1945 and other specified related laws.

Section 2. The President shall terminate U.S. membership in the United Nations (U.N.), including any organ, specialized agency, commission, or other formally affiliated body.

Section 3. The President shall close the U.S. Mission to the United Nations.

Section 4. The following shall hereafter be unlawful: a) Any funds for the U.S. assessed or voluntary contribution to the U.N.; b) Any authorization of funds for any U.S. contribution to any U.N. military or peacekeeping operation; c) Expenditure of funds to support the participation of U.S. Armed Forces as part of any U.N. military or peacekeeping

72

operation; d) U.S. armed forces serving under U.N. command; and d) diplomatic immunity for U.N. officers or employees.

13) The ***Lawful Wars Act***, reiterating Congress' duty to declare wars, repealing the War Powers Resolution of 1973 and barring any administration from initiating foreign hostilities or mobilizing U.S. military in foreign lands without a Declaration of War; requiring Congress to assure that such mobilization or hostilities are necessary to defend against a demonstrable threat to these United States of America.

14) The ***Federal Pork Sunset Act,*** stipulating:

In Fiscal Year 2015, federal government doled out $700 billion in illicit funds to the States, counties, and cities across our republic. The long tradition of such 'pork' projects with strings attached has perverted the citizen's view of his place atop the Constitution's hierarchy and allowed Washington D.C. to assume the role of a master, and the sovereign States and cities, piglets at sow-teats. This criminogenic arrangement has rendered our local, county and State public servants willing to do whatever they must, to receive their share of funds (originating from the people themselves) from countless unaccountable, largely invisible federal agencies. This criminal activity must end.

Section 1. For three (3) fiscal years after passage of this Act, all revenues sent by federal government as grants to States and their subdivisions shall be remitted as a single block grant to each State, with no federal conditions attached, i.e., the States having liberty to determine all uses of said funds.

Section 2. Commencing on the first day of the fourth fiscal year after the date of passage of this Act, any federal grant to a State or subdivision thereof shall be a federal felony.

15) The ***Minuteman Act***, pursuant to Congress's power to "provide for...arming...the Militia" contained in the U.S. Constitution, stipulating:

73

Section 1. The National Firearms Act of 1934, Omnibus Crime Control and Safe Streets Act of 1968, the Gun Control Act of 1968, the Firearm Owners Protection Act of 1986, and the Brady Handgun Violation Prevention Act of 1993 are hereby repealed.

Section 2. No statute, regulation, executive order, or other directive with the purported force of law of federal government, present or future, or that of any State or subdivision thereof, shall infringe on or burden the right of any citizen of, or legal resident alien in, any State who is eligible for membership in that State's Militia to purchase, own, possess, transport, or sell, whether interstate or intrastate, any firearm, ammunition, or related accoutrements suitable for service in a Militia as that term is used in the U.S. Constitution.

Section 3. No statute, regulation, executive order, or other directive with the purported force of law of federal government, present or future, shall infringe on or burden, except on the same terms as apply to any other business, the right of any person to engage in the commercial design, manufacture, repair, sale and distribution, or other trade or occupation involving firearms, ammunition, and Militia accoutrements.

Section 4. As stipulated in Article I, Section 8, Clause 15 of the U.S. Constitution, the several States retain the power to enforce this legislation by appropriate State legislation and duly authorized Citizen Militia enforcement within their respective jurisdictions and subdivisions.

16) The ***Non-Conscription Act***, stipulating:

Section 1. Neither Congress nor any president or federal court has the power to conscript Americans of any age into involuntary national service or servitude of any kind.

Section 2. As stipulated in Article I, Section 8, Clause 15 of the U.S. Constitution, the several States retain the power to enforce this legislation by appropriate State legislation and duly authorized Citizen Militia enforcement within their respective jurisdictions.

17) The ***Return of Sovereign Lands Act***, stipulating:

Section 1. Upon acceptance as a sovereign State of these United States, all lands and resources within said State become the sovereign property of the American People living within said State, and the individual right to private property is no more sacred than the collective right of sovereign property for every sovereign government on earth. The federal government has no lawful authority or claim of sovereignty over – or claim to minerals or other natural resources in, on or under – any land on earth, except as stipulated in Article I, Section 8, Clause 17 of the U.S. Constitution.

Section 2. No sale of any land or resource within any of the sovereign States shall be made by the U.S. government or any entity thereof on behalf of said government, effective immediately, except such surface land as stipulated in Article I, Section 8, Clause 17 of the U.S. Constitution.

Section 3. The United States government shall, within 24 months of the passage of this Act, relinquish all claims to, or jurisdiction in, all sovereign places other than those lands specifically stipulated in Article I, Section 8, Clause 17 of the U.S. Constitution as being within the exclusive legislative domain of Congress.

*Section 4. The federal government has no constitutional authority to **seize** private or State sovereign land, water, timber, oil, gas, minerals, or other natural resources in, on, or under such land in any State, for any reason, under any conditions.*

Section 5. Other than purchases from the States for military installations, federal government has no constitutional auth-

75

*ority to **accept** lands or resources via a State constitution or legislative act.*

Section 6. As to purchases from the sovereign States for military installations, federal government has constitutional authority to purchase lands in a State only with "Consent of the Legislature of the State in which the Same shall be". Said consent of the State Legislature must be accompanied by a majority-vote approval of the People of that State via single-issue referendum or plebiscite.

Section 7. All present federally claimed, held, or controlled lands and any minerals, water, forests and timber, or any other resource within each sovereign State shall revert within 24 months to full control and ownership of the State in which it is located, to be managed and controlled as the People of that State shall determine. The costs of transferring control of formerly federally-claimed lands and natural resources shall be borne by the State in which said lands and resources are located.

Section 8. All federal land-use regulations, national forest and park acts, and like federal controls, restrictions, and prohibitions that deprive private owners of the full use and enjoyment of their private properties pursuant to the laws of the several States, shall be repealed within 12 months of passage of this Act.

Section 9. As reparations for the past federal use and control of sovereign State lands, all federal government improvements, fixtures, facilities, equipment, vehicles and other appurtenances located within each sovereign State (except on military installations) shall become the property of that State, effective immediately. The legal transfer of all said public property located within each State shall be administered by the government of that State, and shall include executive, legislative and judicial branches and Citizen Militia as applicable.

Section 10. Congress shall provide to the sovereign People of the United States, within 12 months of passage of this Act, its detailed plan to relinquish control of all foreign military bases and to cease funding for, and operations of, all foreign land-based military and civil government operations, transferring foreign civil governance to the governments or people of those sovereign lands, within 36 months of the passage of this Act.

Section 11. Irrespective of any local independence movements within sovereign foreign lands outside the 50 states of these United States, all noncontiguous, foreign, and/or 'U.S. possession' claims shall revert to the full, un-fettered control of the peoples of those sovereign lands at their own expense and with no additional expense borne by American citizens after 24 months from passage of this Act.

18) The ***Lawful United States Money and Banking Act*** which will contain elements of, but be more comprehensive than H.R. 459, 833, 1094, 1095, 1098, 1496 and 2768 and SB 202, stipulating at least the following:

Section 1. The American people have delegated the power to 'coin Money' only to Congress, and have delegated to Congress only the power to 'coin' Money.

Section 2. Congress lacks any authority to delegate or to fail, neglect, or refuse to exercise this power.

Section 3. The Legal Tender Act of 1862, the Federal Reserve Act of 1913, and all subsequent amendments of those acts, have been unconstitutional since their enactment.

Section 4. The special privileges now attaching to Federal Reserve Notes— that such notes shall be redeemed in lawful money by the United States Department of the Treasury, shall be receivable for all taxes and other public dues, and shall be legal tender for all debts, public and private—have since enactment been in violation of our Supreme Law.

Section 5. As remedies for these violations of the Constitution, Congress shall establish as an alternative to the Federal Reserve System and Federal Reserve Notes, a system of official money consisting solely of gold and silver, with silver coins to be valued in 'dollars' at the prevailing exchange rate between silver and gold in the free market.

Section 6. This new, lawful U.S. money shall be produced through immediate free coinage of whatever gold and silver may be brought to the United States Mints; including sale of the existing national gold stocks, replaced by silver stock if the gold-silver ratio suggests silver as preferable for the initial coinage.

Section 7. Said reserves and coinage and/or fully-convertible paper or electronic receipts for physical gold and silver, shall be substituted for Federal Reserve Notes as rapidly as maintenance of stability throughout America's economy will permit, in all financial transactions of the general government.

Section 8. The Federal Reserve Act of 1913 (as amended) shall be further amended such that: a) after the effective date of such legislation, the Federal Reserve System shall have no official relationship to the general government, and b) Federal Reserve regional banks shall obtain new charters from the States consistent with the laws thereof or cease doing business as of the date on which the Secretary of the Treasury shall certify that all financial transactions of federal government are being conducted solely in gold and silver or fully-convertible paper or electronic receipts for physical gold and silver.

Section 9. The States have always enjoyed the right as sovereign governments and a duty pursuant to Article I, Section 10 of the Constitution to employ gold and silver coin or fully-convertible paper or electronic receipts for physical gold and silver, to the exclusion of any other currency as their medium of exchange in their sovereign functions.

Neither Congress, nor the president, nor any court, nor any international or supra-national body, nor any private parties have authority to require a State to employ anything other than gold and silver coin or fully-convertible paper or electronic receipts for physical gold and silver.

Section 10. The practice of fractional reserve banking is to be ended within 12 months of the passage of this legislation, and all American financial institutions shall be required to maintain in their vaults 100% reserves against loans made. Any financial institution accepting deposits in the normal course of business, that is unable to pay on demand all such deposits in gold and/or silver or fully-convertible paper or electronic receipts for physical gold and silver, the directors, officers, shareholders, partners, trustees, or other owners and managers of said institution shall be personally liable (their own personal assets subject to seizure) to satisfy unpaid deposit balances under the laws of the State in which the demand for payment of such balances is made.

Section 11. It shall be a federal felony for any person to enact or enforce any tax or financial burden on: a) any exchange of one form of United States money for another form of money thereof, notwithstanding that the nominal value of one form may be different than the nominal value of the other form involved in the transaction; or b) the movement of privately-owned United States money by any private citizen, to or from the United States to or from any other domicile that said private citizen may desire, provided said funds are not being demonstrably used in, or do not demonstrably result from, illegal activity.

Section 12. This legislation shall apply to Federal Reserve Notes, base-metallic and debased silver coinage, and all paper currencies of the United States until the date on which the Secretary of the Treasury shall certify that all federal financial transactions are being conducted solely in gold and silver or fully-convertible paper or electronic receipts for

*physical gold and silver, and thereafter only as Congress
shall determine necessary.*

19) The ***Intelligent Republic Act,*** a reform law based very
loosely on the Smart Nation Act, sponsored by Congressman
Rob Simmons (R-CT), must provide for orderly dismantling
and defunding of all secret intelligence operations by federal
government as recommended by former CIA officers Kevin
Shipp and Robert David Steele.

The National Security Act of 1947 created the CIA and the
National Security Council, which is accountable only to
presidents. Congress, which represents the People and the
States, allowed itself no oversight of the NSC. That criminal
act of legislation never defined or limited what the CIA can or
cannot do, and did not authorize covert operations closed to
congressional oversight.

Even if the House Permanent Select Committee on
Intelligence and the Senate Select Committee on Intelligence
attempted to de-fund the most egregious crimes of this
criminal agency, the CIA makes this impossible. First, it
makes all of its budget line items and appropriations
classified, keeping its operations secret from Congress thus
making it impossible to de-fund the agency in part.

Second, the CIA maintains blackmail dossiers on all members
of Congress so that no legislator would dare reduce that
criminal organization's programs or funding. Thus, this
criminal operation must be dismantled, outlawed, and de-
funded *in full.*

With illicit funding generated by foreign drug operations,
these criminal agencies give U.S. presidents and even agency
underlings, power over foreign governments.

Secret agencies unaccountable to the American people are
unconstitutional and have increasingly destructive impact on
American security, liberty, and public morale. It is clearly
unconstitutional for federal government to create foreign

operating agencies, fund private offshore contractors, or create alliances with foreign countries, whether for intelligence or supposed 'defense'. Such corrupt traditions violate the U.S. Constitution by usurping the authority of Congress and the Citizen Militia.

The Constitution stipulates that the Citizen Militia shall *"execute the Laws of the Union, suppress Insurrections, and repel Invasions"*. Thus, all networks, cells, and offices for intelligence in the American republic must operate under a local aegis of the Citizen Militia and are ultimately the duty and authority of the People, and accountable to the People.

Each unit of Citizen Militia, according to the Constitution, is to follow *"the discipline prescribed by Congress"*, with officers appointed by and training/equipment/logistics supplied by its State legislature.

* * *

We The People reserve the right to revise and extend the list of federal government arrogations, violations, and usurpations brought to our attention for remediation by AmericaAgain! members via our State courts and through reform legislation.

Should our member of Congress or State legislator refuse to cease violating the law; should he prevaricate and bloviate as politicians often do, or conspire anew with like-minded scoundrels and moneyed oligarchs who purchased his first allegiance – we will seek his criminal conviction in State Court, the longest possible State Penitentiary term, and as actual and punitive damages for massive fraud and conspiracy, we will seek to have our State Court seize all assets held under any structure whatsoever, in any jurisdiction whatsoever, inuring to his benefit or that of his family or descendants.

Any state prosecutor, district attorney, judge, constable, sheriff or other state public servant who refuses to oversee justice as his oath of office demands, may become the target of a State Grand Jury, jointly deploying as needed with its corresponding constitutional Militia.

Appendix B

28th Amendment Fact Sheet

Text of the 1789 Amendment

Article the First. – After the First Enumeration, required by the First Article of the Constitution, there shall be One Representative for every Thirty Thousand, until the Number shall amount to One Hundred; after which the Proportion shall be so regulated by Congress that there shall not be less than One Hundred Representatives, nor less than One Representative for every Forty Thousand Persons, until the number of Representatives shall amount to Two Hundred, after which the Proportion shall be so regulated by Congress that there shall not be less than Two Hundred Representatives, nor more than one Representative for every Fifty Thousand Persons.

Q: If we ratify this 28th Amendment with a U.S. population of 320 million, we'll have 6,400 members of the U.S. House! Where would we put them all?

A: Which government places greater burdens on the American people – State or federal? The same 320 million Americans have 7,382 *state* legislators but only 535 federal ones? This is preposterous.

After ratifying the amendment, during the massive redistricting process in every state, AmericaAgain! will be

pushing passage of the *Bring Congress Home Act* (BCHA) –
a far more comprehensive version of HR287 filed by Eric
Swalwell (D-CA) and Steve Pearce (R-NM) in 2013.
Congress must move out of the 19th century.

Q: But won't the added cost be astronomical?

A: Total congressional operating budget would be
approximately equal to the present $5.85 billion. Rather than
the present 3-6 offices and staffs, U.S. congressmen under the
BCHA would have a single office and paid staff of two. The
BCHA will also end opulent perks and pensions and limit all
members of Congress to two terms, either house.

Q: Doesn't the 20th Amendment say, "The Congress shall
assemble at least once in every year, and such meeting shall
begin at noon on the 3rd day of January"?

A: Yes. People attend meetings every day via teleconference
and videoconference; Congress can do the same. It's time
We The People ended Washington D.C. organized crime, and
we begin with the 28th Amendment.

Q: It has been 223 years since the last ratification vote was
held on this original First Amendment; hasn't the statute of
limitations run out on this process?

A: No; unless there is a ratification deadline in the body of
the article, a constitutional amendment has no expiration date
for ratification. The original Second Amendment was not
finally ratified by the required 38th state legislature until 204
years after Congress passed it on to the states for ratification
in 1789.

Q: If this amendment was so important, it would have been ratified when Congress first passed it.

A: It _was_ ratified when Congress first passed it! See page 3 of the draft Joint Resolution; the Connecticut House of Representatives in October 1789 voted to ratify; the CT Senate in May 1790 also voted to ratify. The House sought in 1790 to alter its vote due to a transcribing error, but the Senate rejected the idea, thus technically, Kentucky's 1792 vote was the twelfth vote among 15 states, more than three-fourths of the states.

Q: With 6400 seats in the U.S. House, we will be faced with a massive redistricting project. Given our workload on budgetary and operational matters in our state, why should the State Legislature spend time on this frivolous political issue?

A: George Washington did not speak publicly at the 1787 Constitutional Convention until the final day of that historic four-month gathering. When he finally rose to speak on the last day of the convention, Washington's first words were to urge his fellow delegates to support apportionment of representation at one congressman per 30,000 people. As a practical matter, this is very simple: no committees, reconciliation bill, or governor's signature for a ratification vote, and we provided your draft Joint Resolution. This is not rocket science.

As to redistricting your state for proper apportionment of U.S. representatives, AmericaAgain! has contracted a GIS mapping company and redistricting attorneys who will work with your legislature's designated staff and/or redistricting committee to help draw final boundaries and GIS/TIGER maps for your state's new U.S. congressional districts, at no charge to the taxpayers (up to three district map and data set iterations).

Q. Some people argue that the amendment has a fatal flaw in the last sentence, *"there shall not be less than Two Hundred Representatives, nor **more** than one Representative for every Fifty Thousand Persons."* That should say, not less than one for every 50,000 persons; so if we ratify, we could have as few as 200 members in the U.S. House. How do you answer these websites?

A. Read the amendment; as the 11 legislatures knew when they ratified the amendment, it is clear that the progression is 1: 30,000 then 1: 40,000 and finally 1: 50,000 people. Those who raise this objection either have ulterior motives or are ignorant of the history of Article I, Section 2, Clause 4.

The 71st Congress, in restricting the House to only 435 districts, hijacked the Constitution. As explained on page 5 of the book *FEAR The People,* the Founding Fathers made this their first article of amendment because, as George Washington made clear during the Convention, adequate representation was paramount. It is time for our state legislatures to turn the tables on Washington D.C., bring Congress home, and restore rule of law.

This first vital step in that process cannot be stopped by Washington D.C.; the amendment was passed by Congress, sent on to the state legislatures, and arguably already ratified once. **Now it is *your* duty to perform!**

Appendix C

Model Joint Resolution

House Joint Resolution
Original Constitutional Amendment #1
(28th Amendment)
Offered by Rep. _____

WHEREAS, The First Congress of the United States of America, at its first session begun and held March 4, 1789, sitting in New York, New York, in both houses, by a constitutional majority of two-thirds thereof, adopted the following proposition to amend the Constitution of the United States of America in the following words, to wit:

"RESOLVED, by the Senate and House of Representatives of the United States of America in Congress assembled, two thirds of both houses concurring, that the following (Article) be proposed to the Legislatures of the several States, ... which (Article), when ratified by three fourths of the said Legislatures, to be valid to all intents and purposes, as part of the said Constitution, viz.: (An Article) in addition to, and Amendment of the Constitution of the United States of America, proposed by Congress, and ratified by the Legislatures of the several States, pursuant to the fifth Article of the original Constitution.

"Article the First. – After the First Enumeration, required by the First Article of the Constitution, there shall be One Representative for every Thirty Thousand, until the Number shall amount to One Hundred; after which the Proportion shall be so regulated by Congress that there shall not be less

87

than One Hundred Representatives, nor less than One Representative for every Forty Thousand Persons, until the number of Representatives shall amount to Two Hundred, after which the Proportion shall be so regulated by Congress that there shall not be less than Two Hundred Representatives, nor more than one Representative for every Fifty Thousand Persons." And

WHEREAS, on the last day of the 1787 Constitutional Convention, delegate Nathanael Gorham proposed a change in Article I, Section 2, Clause 4 of the new U.S. Constitution, to limit the size of a U.S. congressional district to 30,000 people rather than 40,000 people – and this was the only subject about which President George Washington felt strongly enough to publicly address the Convention, urging the revision to smaller districts because 40,000 was too large; and

WHEREAS, of the first 12 amendments passed by Congress on September 25, 1789 the subject amendment was placed in first position for the reason given by Melancton Smith at the New York ratifying convention: *"We certainly ought to fix in the Constitution those things which are essential to liberty. If anything falls under this description, it is the number of the legislature"*; and

WHEREAS in one of the Anti-Federalist letters, the prophetic 'Cato' admonished: *"It is a very important objection to this government, that the representation consists of so few; too few to resist the influence of corruption, and the temptation to treachery, against which all governments ought to take precautions…"* and

WHEREAS, Article V of the Constitution of the United States allows the ratification of the proposed Amendment to the United States Constitution by the Legislature of the State

88

of _____ , and does not dictate a time limit on ratification of an amendment submitted by Congress, and the First Congress specifically having not provided a time constraint for ratification of the above-quoted Amendment; and

WHEREAS, The Supreme Court of the United States in 1939 ruled in the landmark case of Coleman v. Miller that Congress is the final arbiter on the question of whether too much time has elapsed between Congress' submission of a particular amendment and the most recent state legislature's ratification of same if Congress did not specify a deadline on the proposal's consideration; and

WHEREAS, the Legislature of the State of _____ finds that the proposed Amendment is today even more meaningful and necessary to the United States Constitution than in the eighteenth century when submitted for adoption, given the level of corruption and lobbyist tampering resulting in multi-million-dollar U.S. congressional elections and inability of the United States Representative to meaningfully interact with the citizens he or she is supposed to represent; and

WHEREAS, the original First Amendment was designed to avoid precisely what we suffer today: multimillion-dollar campaigns for U.S. congressmen whose districts include up to 750,000 citizens and more – a population that they can never personally know, much less represent; and

WHEREAS, the proposed amendment to the United States Constitution has already been ratified by the legislatures of the following 11 states on the dates indicated, to wit: New Jersey on November 20, 1789; Maryland on December 19, 1789; North Carolina on December 22, 1789; South Carolina on January 19, 1790; New Hampshire on January 25, 1790;

New York on March 27, 1790; Rhode Island on June 15, 1790; Pennsylvania on September 21, 1791; Vermont on November 3, 1791; Virginia on December 15, 1791; and Kentucky on June 24, 1792; and

WHEREAS, the original First Amendment did actually receive sufficient votes for ratification once Kentucky's vote was recorded, due to the fact that the Connecticut House of Representatives in October 1789 voted to ratify Article the First, and the Connecticut Senate in May 1790 also voted to ratify it, and although the House sought by May 1790 to alter its vote due to a transcribing error, the Senate rejected the idea, thus technically, Kentucky's 1792 vote was the twelfth vote in 15 states at the time, the original First Amendment thus having been ratified by more than three-fourths of the states, making this present-day campaign truly a *re-ratification* of the People's original Right in the Bill of Rights; and

WHEREAS in 1993, the thirty-eighth State Legislature ratified the original Second Amendment, which had been ratified by the first State over 204 years earlier, at which time the Archivist of the United States declared it ratified as the Twenty-Seventh Amendment to the United States Constitution; and

WHEREAS this joint resolution only calls for the ratification vote of the original First Amendment to the U.S. Constitution under the stipulations of Article V thereof, and is not state legislation requiring committee deliberations, a reconciliation process or signature by the Governor; and

WHEREAS all due deliberation on this matter has been held on the floor of both Houses of this Legislature, it was found in the best interests of the people of _____ that the ratification vote be held without delay, and such vote having been held in favor of ratification;

THEREFORE, be it RESOLVED, BY THE HOUSE OF REPRESENTATIVES OF THE _____ LEGISLATURE OF THE STATE OF _____, THE SENATE CONCURRING HEREIN, that the foregoing proposed Amendment to the Constitution of the United States is ratified by the Legislature of the State of _____; and be it further RESOLVED, that the Secretary of State of _____ shall transmit certified copies of this resolution to the Archivist of the United States, to the Vice-President of the United States, and to the Speaker of the United States House of Representatives with a request that it be printed in full in the Congressional Record.

Appendix D

Cost of Congress (Before & After)

Considering how much Americans love to complain about how much our corrupt servants spend over there in D.C., it's amazing to realize that we're probably the only employers on the face of the earth who allow our employees to write their own ticket. As we explained earlier in this book, each member of Congress spends on his own office and personal operations, over $10.9 million annually. Can you imagine spending that much just to supposedly represent your boss who never checks in on you, never audits your expenses, and has no idea of the opulence of your meals, limousines, private jets, spas, hairstylists, and even of your legal settlements with young ladies you attempted to fondle or rape?

That's the U.S. Congress today. No wonder every sleazebag in America aspires to a government job.

Okay, so now the Boss is angry; we're going to put our foot down and split them up into small districts, then bring them home under permanent probation. We plan to get these thousands of new candidates (we refer to them as TACTICAL CIVICS™ Good Guys) to agree to live a totally different lifestyle back home: we have their operation audited yearly, and we cut their salary (congressmen, not senators) in half and end all benefits. This is not meant to be a career; only a short-term gig, representing your neighbors.

People kept telling us that 6,400 congressmen would spend ten times more than 435 of them. But that's nonsense; here are the numbers for a typical congressman (member of the U.S. House)…

U.S. House Member- Proposed Operating Budget

(After breaking up the House into small districts, and passing the Bring Congress Home Act)

Currently, Congress spends $5.85 billion on its own operations; $10,934,579 *per member!*

Member Operations Reasonable Budget (Item Description)	Annual
Legislator $98,000 salary plus 40% burden	$137,200
Senior staffer (ofc manager) $65,000 salary plus 40% burden	$91,000
Junior staffer, research & clerical $45,000 salary plus 40% burden	$63,000
Office rent ($5000/mo)	$60,000
Utilities ($750/mo)	$9,000
Phone & Internet service ($1500/mo)	$18,000
Publications (no mailing; website only, plus PDF) allow $3,000/mo	$36,000
Research expenses and publications ($5,000/mo)	$60,000
Copying services (for legislative and other publications; $5,000/mo)	$60,000
Legislative drafting services ($5,000/mo)	$60,000
Computer systems support ($500/mo)	$6,000
Website maintenance ($400/mo)	$4,800
Insurance (fire/theft/casualty; $500/mo)	$6,000
Very limited travel (because this is where secret deal-cutting takes place!)	$25,000
Office supplies, furniture rental ($3,000/mo)	$36,000
(4) computer systems (one for the People testifying before committees)	$14,000
Alarm & security services ($750/mo)	$9,000
Gasoline allowance (to attend events only in the district; $500/mo)	$6,000
Auditor selected by the People of the district ($1500/mo)	$18,000
Total Budget (less contingencies)	$719,000
Contingencies (10%) audited and posted quarterly on website	$71,900
Total Proposed Operating Budget	**$790,900**

Now with 6,400 congressmen each getting $791,000 that's a total of $5,062,400,000. Remember that total; now let's look at our new budget for U.S. senators' operations…

U.S. Senator- Proposed Operating Budget

(After breaking up the House into small districts, and passing the Bring Congress Home Act)

Currently, Congress spends $5.85 billion on its own operations; $10,934,579 *per member!*

Member Operations Reasonable Budget (Item Description)	Annual
Legislator $220,000 salary plus 40% burden	$308,000
Senior staffer (ofc manager) $90,000 salary plus 40% burden	$126,000
(5) Junior staffers: research & clerical $55,000 salary plus 40% burden	$385,000
Office rent ($7000/mo)	$84,000
Utilities ($900/mo)	$10,800
Phone & Internet service ($3000/mo)	$36,000
Publications (no mailing; website only, plus PDF) allow $6,000/mo	$72,000
Research expenses and publications ($7,500/mo)	$90,000
Copying services (for legislative and other publications; $8,000/mo)	$96,000
Legislative drafting services ($7,500/mo)	$90,000
Computer systems support ($1000/mo)	$12,000
Website maintenance ($800/mo)	$9,600
Insurance (fire/theft/casualty; $750/mo)	$9,000
Travel	$50,000
Office supplies, furniture rental ($5,000/mo)	$60,000
(8) computer systems (one for the People testifying before committees)	$28,000
Alarm & security services ($1000/mo)	$12,000
Gasoline allowance (to attend events; $800/mo)	$9,600
Auditor selected by the People of the district ($2500/mo)	$30,000
Total Budget (less contingencies)	$1,518,000
Contingencies (10%) audited and posted quarterly on website	$151,800
Total Proposed Operating Budget	**$1,669,800**

With 100 senators at $1,670,000 each that's a total of $167 million annually; so $5,062,400,000 plus $167,000,000 equals a total of $5,229,400,000. Imagine: even with 14 times more congressmen, we can save $621 million per year by making Congress work back home in modest offices, ending the opulence and embezzlement they lavish on themselves in D.C. while we pay the bills!

It's time for the Bring Congress Home Act. But first we have to get those 27 state legislatures to hold their ratification vote on our First Right.

Appendix E

The U.S. Constitution

*This edition of the Constitution contains the exact language of the original, including archaic spellings. For ease of reference, we have added an indexing system, appearing before each clause in bold numerals. For instance, Article I, Section 8, Clause 15 reads, "**1.8.15** To provide for calling forth the Militia to execute the Laws of the Union, suppress Insurrections and repel Invasions".*

This indexing system developed by Michael Holler allows the citizen to quickly reference and more easily memorize any clause of the Constitution.

We The People of the United States, in Order to form a more perfect Union, establish Justice, insure domestic Tranquility, provide for the common defence, promote the general Welfare, and secure the Blessings of Liberty to ourselves and our Posterity, do ordain and establish this Constitution for the United States of America.

Article I
Section 1

All legislative Powers herein granted shall be vested in a Congress of the United States, which shall consist of a Senate and House of Representatives.

Section 2

1.2.1   The House of Representatives shall be composed of Members chosen every second Year by the People of the several States, and the Electors in each State shall have the Qualifications requisite for Electors of the most numerous Branch of the State Legislature.

1.2.2   No Person shall be a Representative who shall not have attained to the Age of twenty five Years, and been seven Years a Citizen of the United States, and who shall not, when elected, be an Inhabitant of that State in which he shall be chosen.

1.2.3   Representatives and direct Taxes shall be apportioned among the several States which may be included within this Union, according to their respective Numbers, which shall be determined by adding to the whole Number of free Persons, including those bound to Service for a Term of Years, and excluding Indians not taxed, three fifths of all other Persons.

1.2.4   The actual Enumeration shall be made within three Years after the first Meeting of the Congress of the United States, and within every subsequent Term of ten Years, in such Manner as they shall by Law direct. The Number of Representatives shall not exceed one for every thirty Thousand, but each State shall have at Least one Representative; and until such enumeration shall be made, the State of New Hampshire shall be entitled to chuse three, Massachusetts eight, Rhode-Island and Providence Plantations one, Connecticut five, New-York six, New Jersey four, Pennsylvania eight, Delaware one, Maryland six, Virginia ten, North Carolina five, South Carolina five, and Georgia three.

1.2.5 When vacancies happen in the Representation from any State, the Executive Authority thereof shall issue Writs of Election to fill such Vacancies.

1.2.6 The House of Representatives shall chuse their Speaker and other Officers; and shall have the sole Power of Impeachment.

Section 3

1.3.1 The Senate of the United States shall be composed of two Senators from each State, chosen by the Legislature thereof, for six Years; and each Senator shall have one Vote.

1.3.2 Immediately after they shall be assembled in Consequence of the first Election, they shall be divided as equally as may be into three Classes. The Seats of the Senators of the first Class shall be vacated at the Expiration of the second Year, of the second Class at the Expiration of the fourth Year, and of the third Class at the Expiration of the sixth Year, so that one third may be chosen every second Year;

1.3.3 and if Vacancies happen by Resignation, or otherwise, during the Recess of the Legislature of any State, the Executive thereof may make temporary Appointments until the next Meeting of the Legislature, which shall then fill such Vacancies.

1.3.4 No Person shall be a Senator who shall not have attained to the Age of thirty Years, and been nine Years a Citizen of the United States, and who shall not, when elected, be an Inhabitant of that State for which he shall be chosen.

1.3.5 The Vice President of the United States shall be President of the Senate, but shall have no Vote, unless they be equally divided.

1.3.6 The Senate shall chuse their other Officers, and also a President pro tempore, in the Absence of the Vice President, or when he shall exercise the Office of President of the United States.

1.3.7 The Senate shall have the sole Power to try all Impeachments. When sitting for that Purpose, they shall be on Oath or Affirmation. When the President of the United States is tried, the Chief Justice shall preside: And no Person shall be convicted without the Concurrence of two thirds of the Members present.

1.3.8 Judgment in Cases of Impeachment shall not extend further than to removal from Office, and disqualification to hold and enjoy any Office of honor, Trust or Profit under the United States: but the Party convicted shall nevertheless be liable and subject to Indictment, Trial, Judgment and Punishment, according to Law.

Section 4

1.4.1 The Times, Places and Manner of holding Elections for Senators and Representatives, shall be prescribed in each State by the Legislature thereof; but the Congress may at any time by Law make or alter such Regulations, except as to the Places of chusing Senators.

1.4.2 The Congress shall assemble at least once in every Year, and such Meeting shall be on the first Monday in December, unless they shall by Law appoint a different Day. [Changed; see 20th Amendment.]

Section 5

1.5.1   Each House shall be the Judge of the Elections, Returns and Qualifications of its own Members, and a Majority of each shall constitute a Quorum to do Business; but a smaller Number may adjourn from day to day, and may be authorized to compel the Attendance of absent Members, in such Manner, and under such Penalties as each House may provide.

1.5.2   Each House may determine the Rules of its Proceedings, punish its Members for disorderly Behaviour, and, with the Concurrence of two thirds, expel a Member.

1.5.3   Each House shall keep a Journal of its Proceedings, and from time to time publish the same, excepting such Parts as may in their Judgment require Secrecy; and the Yeas and Nays of the Members of either House on any question shall, at the Desire of one fifth of those Present, be entered on the Journal.

1.5.4   Neither House, during the Session of Congress, shall, without the Consent of the other, adjourn for more than three days, nor to any other Place than that in which the two Houses shall be sitting.

Section 6

1.6.1   The Senators and Representatives shall receive a Compensation for their Services, to be ascertained by Law, and paid out of the Treasury of the United States.

1.6.2   They shall in all Cases, except Treason, Felony and Breach of the Peace, be privileged from Arrest during their Attendance at the Session of their respective Houses, and in going to and returning from the same; and for any Speech or

Debate in either House, they shall not be questioned in any other Place.

1.6.3 No Senator or Representative shall, during the Time for which he was elected, be appointed to any civil Office under the Authority of the United States, which shall have been created, or the Emoluments whereof shall have been encreased during such time; and no Person holding any Office under the United States, shall be a Member of either House during his Continuance in Office.

Section 7

1.7.1 All Bills for raising Revenue shall originate in the House of Representatives; but the Senate may propose or concur with Amendments as on other Bills.

1.7.2 Every Bill which shall have passed the House of Representatives and the Senate, shall, before it become a Law, be presented to the President of the United States; If he approve he shall sign it, but if not he shall return it, with his Objections to that House in which it shall have originated, who shall enter the Objections at large on their Journal, and proceed to reconsider it.

1.7.3 If after such Reconsideration two thirds of that House shall agree to pass the Bill, it shall be sent, together with the Objections, to the other House, by which it shall likewise be reconsidered, and if approved by two thirds of that House, it shall become a Law.

1.7.4 But in all such Cases the Votes of both Houses shall be determined by yeas and Nays, and the Names of the Persons voting for and against the Bill shall be entered on the Journal of each House respectively. If any Bill shall not be returned by the President within ten Days (Sundays excepted) after it shall have been presented to him, the Same shall be a Law, in like Manner as if he had signed it, unless the Congress by their Adjournment prevent its Return, in which Case it shall not be a Law.

1.7.5 Every Order, Resolution, or Vote to which the Concurrence of the Senate and House of Representatives may be necessary (except on a question of Adjournment) shall be presented to the President of the United States; and before the Same shall take Effect, shall be approved by him, or being disapproved by him, shall be repassed by two thirds of the Senate and House of Representatives, according to the Rules and Limitations prescribed in the Case of a Bill.

Section 8

1.8.1 The Congress shall have Power To lay and collect Taxes, Duties, Imposts and Excises, to pay the Debts and provide for the common Defence and general Welfare of the United States; but all Duties, Imposts and Excises shall be uniform throughout the United States;

1.8.2 To borrow Money on the credit of the United States;

1.8.3 To regulate Commerce with foreign Nations, and among the several States, and with the Indian Tribes;

1.8.4 To establish an uniform Rule of Naturalization, and uniform Laws on the subject of Bankruptcies throughout the United States;

1.8.5 To coin Money, regulate the Value thereof, and of foreign Coin, and fix the Standard of Weights and Measures;

1.8.6 To provide for the Punishment of counterfeiting the Securities and current Coin of the United States;

1.8.7 To establish Post Offices and post Roads;

1.8.8 To promote the Progress of Science and useful Arts, by securing for limited Times to Authors and Inventors the exclusive Right to their respective Writings and Discoveries;

1.8.9 To constitute Tribunals inferior to the supreme Court;

1.8.10 To define and punish Piracies and Felonies committed on the high Seas, and Offences against the Law of Nations;

1.8.11 To declare War, grant Letters of Marque and Reprisal, and make Rules concerning Captures on Land and Water;

1.8.12 To raise and support Armies, but no Appropriation of Money to that Use shall be for a longer Term than two Years;

1.8.13 To provide and maintain a Navy;

1.8.14 To make Rules for the Government and Regulation of the land and naval Forces;

1.8.15 To provide for calling forth the Militia to execute the Laws of the Union, suppress Insurrections and repel Invasions;

1.8.16 To provide for organizing, arming, and disciplining, the Militia, and for governing such Part of them as may be employed in the Service of the United States, reserving to the States respectively, the Appointment of the Officers, and the Authority of training the Militia according to the discipline prescribed by Congress;

1.8.17   To exercise exclusive Legislation in all Cases whatsoever, over such District (not exceeding ten Miles square) as may, by Cession of particular States, and the Acceptance of Congress, become the Seat of the Government of the United States, and to exercise like Authority over all Places purchased by the Consent of the Legislature of the State in which the Same shall be, for the Erection of Forts, Magazines, Arsenals, dock-Yards, and other needful Buildings;—And

1.8.18   To make all Laws which shall be necessary and proper for carrying into Execution the foregoing Powers, and all other Powers vested by this Constitution in the Government of the United States, or in any Department or Officer thereof.

Section 9

1.9.1   The Migration or Importation of such Persons as any of the States now existing shall think proper to admit, shall not be prohibited by the Congress prior to the Year one thousand eight hundred and eight, but a Tax or duty may be imposed on such Importation, not exceeding ten dollars for each Person. [Nullified; now obsolete.]

1.9.2   The Privilege of the Writ of Habeas Corpus shall not be suspended, unless when in Cases of Rebellion or Invasion the public Safety may require it.

1.9.3   No Bill of Attainder or ex post facto Law shall be passed.

1.9.4   No Capitation, or other direct, Tax shall be laid, unless in Proportion to the Census or enumeration herein before directed to be taken.

1.9.5   No Tax or Duty shall be laid on Articles exported from any State.

1.9.6   No Preference shall be given by any Regulation of Commerce or Revenue to the Ports of one State over those of another: nor shall Vessels bound to, or from, one State, be obliged to enter, clear, or pay Duties in another.

1.9.7   No Money shall be drawn from the Treasury, but in Consequence of Appropriations made by Law; and a regular Statement and Account of the Receipts and Expenditures of all public Money shall be published from time to time.

1.9.8   No Title of Nobility shall be granted by the United States: And no Person holding any Office of Profit or Trust under them, shall, without the Consent of the Congress, accept of any present, Emolument, Office, or Title, of any kind whatever, from any King, Prince, or foreign State.

Section 10

1.10.1   No State shall enter into any Treaty, Alliance, or Confederation; grant Letters of Marque and Reprisal;

1.10.2   coin Money; emit Bills of Credit; make any Thing but gold and silver Coin a Tender in Payment of Debts;

1.10.3   pass any Bill of Attainder, ex post facto Law,

1.10.4   or Law impairing the Obligation of Contracts, or grant any Title of Nobility.

1.10.5   No State shall, without the Consent of the Congress, lay any Imposts or Duties on Imports or Exports, except what may be absolutely necessary for executing it's inspection Laws: and the net Produce of all Duties and Imposts, laid by any State on Imports or Exports, shall be for the Use of the Treasury of the United States; and all such Laws shall be subject to the Revision and Controul of the Congress.

1.10.6   No State shall, without the Consent of Congress, lay any Duty of Tonnage, keep Troops, or Ships of War in time of Peace, enter into any Agreement or Compact with another State, or with a foreign Power, or engage in War, unless actually invaded, or in such imminent Danger as will not admit of delay.

Article II

Section 1

2.1.1   The executive Power shall be vested in a President of the United States of America. He shall hold his Office during the Term of four Years, and, together with the Vice President, chosen for the same Term, be elected, as follows

2.1.2   Each State shall appoint, in such Manner as the Legislature thereof may direct, a Number of Electors, equal to the whole Number of Senators and Representatives to which the State may be entitled in the Congress: but no Senator or Representative, or Person holding an Office of Trust or Profit under the United States, shall be appointed an Elector.

2.1.3   The Electors shall meet in their respective States, and vote by Ballot for two Persons, of whom one at least shall not be an Inhabitant of the same State with themselves.

2.1.4   And they shall make a List of all the Persons voted for, and of the Number of Votes for each; which List they shall sign and certify, and transmit sealed to the Seat of the Government of the United States, directed to the President of the Senate.

2.1.5 The President of the Senate shall, in the Presence of the Senate and House of Representatives, open all the Certificates, and the Votes shall then be counted. The Person having the greatest Number of Votes shall be the President, if such Number be a Majority of the whole Number of Electors appointed;

2.1.6 and if there be more than one who have such Majority, and have an equal Number of Votes, then the House of Representatives shall immediately chuse by Ballot one of them for President; and if no Person have a Majority, then from the five highest on the List the said House shall in like Manner chuse the President. But in chusing the President, the Votes shall be taken by States, the Representation from each State having one Vote; A quorum for this Purpose shall consist of a Member or Members from two thirds of the States, and a Majority of all the States shall be necessary to a Choice. [Changed; see 12th Amendment.]

2.1.7 [Removed; see 20th Amendment.]

2.1.8 [Removed by the 20th Amendment.]

2.1.9 In every Case, after the Choice of the President, the Person having the greatest Number of Votes of the Electors shall be the Vice President. But if there should remain two or more who have equal Votes, the Senate shall chuse from them by Ballot the Vice President. [Changed; see 12th Amendment.]

2.1.10 The Congress may determine the Time of chusing the Electors, and the Day on which they shall give their Votes; which Day shall be the same throughout the United States.

2.1.11 No Person except a natural born Citizen, or a Citizen of the United States, at the time of the Adoption of this Constitution, shall be eligible to the Office of President; neither shall any Person be eligible to that Office who shall not have attained to the Age of thirty five Years, and been fourteen Years a Resident within the United States.

2.1.12 In Case of the Removal of the President from Office, or of his Death, Resignation, or Inability to discharge the Powers and Duties of the said Office, the Same shall devolve on the Vice President, [Changed; see 25th Amendment.]

2.1.13 [See 25th Amendment]

2.1.14 and the Congress may by Law provide for the Case of Removal, Death, Resignation or Inability, both of the President and Vice President, declaring what Officer shall then act as President, and such Officer shall act accordingly, until the Disability be removed, or a President shall be elected.

2.1.15-18 [See 25th Amendment]

2.1.19 The President shall, at stated Times, receive for his Services, a Compensation, which shall neither be encreased nor diminished during the Period for which he shall have been elected, and he shall not receive within that Period any other Emolument from the United States, or any of them.

2.1.20 Before he enter on the Execution of his Office, he shall take the following Oath or Affirmation:—"I do solemnly swear (or affirm) that I will faithfully execute the Office of President of the United States, and will to the best of my Ability, preserve, protect and defend the Constitution of the United States."

Section 2

2.2.1   The President shall be Commander in Chief of the Army and Navy of the United States, and of the Militia of the several States, when called into the actual Service of the United States; he may require the Opinion, in writing, of the principal Officer in each of the executive Departments, upon any Subject relating to the Duties of their respective Offices, and he shall have Power to grant Reprieves and Pardons for Offences against the United States, except in Cases of Impeachment.

2.2.2   He shall have Power, by and with the Advice and Consent of the Senate, to make Treaties, provided two thirds of the Senators present concur; and he shall nominate, and by and with the Advice and Consent of the Senate, shall appoint Ambassadors, other public Ministers and Consuls, Judges of the supreme Court, and all other Officers of the United States, whose Appointments are not herein otherwise provided for, and which shall be established by Law:

2.2.3   but the Congress may by Law vest the Appointment of such inferior Officers, as they think proper, in the President alone, in the Courts of Law, or in the Heads of Departments.

2.2.4   The President shall have Power to fill up all Vacancies that may happen during the Recess of the Senate, by granting Commissions which shall expire at the End of their next Session.

Section 3

2.3.1   He shall from time to time give to the Congress Information of the State of the Union, and recommend to their Consideration such Measures as he shall judge necessary and expedient;

2.3.2 he may, on extraordinary Occasions, convene both Houses, or either of them, and in Case of Disagreement between them, with Respect to the Time of Adjournment, he may adjourn them to such Time as he shall think proper;

2.3.3 he shall receive Ambassadors and other public Ministers; he shall take Care that the Laws be faithfully executed, and shall Commission all the Officers of the United States.

Section 4

The President, Vice President and all civil Officers of the United States, shall be removed from Office on Impeachment for, and Conviction of, Treason, Bribery, or other high Crimes and Misdemeanors.

Article III

Section 1

The judicial Power of the United States, shall be vested in one supreme Court, and in such inferior Courts as the Congress may from time to time ordain and establish. The Judges, both of the supreme and inferior Courts, shall hold their Offices during good Behaviour, and shall, at stated Times, receive for their Services, a Compensation, which shall not be diminished during their Continuance in Office.

Section 2

3.2.1 The judicial Power shall extend to all Cases, in Law and Equity, arising under this Constitution, the Laws of the United States, and Treaties made, or which shall be made, under their Authority;—to all Cases affecting Ambassadors, other public Ministers and Consuls;—to all Cases of admiralty and maritime Jurisdiction;—to Controversies to which the United States shall be a Party;—to Controversies between two or more States;— between a State and Citizens of another State,—between Citizens of different States,— between Citizens of the same State claiming Lands under Grants of different States, and between a State, or the Citizens thereof, and foreign States, Citizens or Subjects. [Changed by the 11th Amendment.]

3.2.2   In all Cases affecting Ambassadors, other public Ministers and Consuls, and those in which a State shall be Party, the supreme Court shall have original Jurisdiction. In all the other Cases before mentioned, the supreme Court shall have appellate Jurisdiction, both as to Law and Fact, with such Exceptions, and under such Regulations as the Congress shall make.

3.2.3   The Trial of all Crimes, except in Cases of Impeachment, shall be by Jury; and such Trial shall be held in the State where the said Crimes shall have been committed; but when not committed within any State, the Trial shall be at such Place or Places as the Congress may by Law have directed.

Section 3

3.3.1 Treason against the United States, shall consist only in levying War against them, or in adhering to their Enemies, giving them Aid and Comfort. No Person shall be convicted of Treason unless on the Testimony of two Witnesses to the same overt Act, or on Confession in open Court.

3.3.2   The Congress shall have Power to declare the Punishment of Treason, but no Attainder of Treason shall work Corruption of Blood, or Forfeiture except during the Life of the Person attainted.

Article IV

Section 1

Full Faith and Credit shall be given in each State to the public Acts, Records, and judicial Proceedings of every other State. And the Congress may by general Laws prescribe the Manner in which such Acts, Records and Proceedings shall be proved, and the Effect thereof.

Section 2

4.2.1   The Citizens of each State shall be entitled to all Privileges and Immunities of Citizens in the several States.

4.2.2   A Person charged in any State with Treason, Felony, or other Crime, who shall flee from Justice, and be found in another State, shall on Demand of the executive Authority of the State from which he fled, be delivered up, to be removed to the State having Jurisdiction of the Crime.

4.2.3   No Person held to Service or Labour in one State, under the Laws thereof, escaping into another, shall, in Consequence of any Law or Regulation therein, be discharged from such Service or Labour, but shall be delivered up on Claim of the Party to whom such Service or Labour may be due. [Made obsolete by the 13th Amendment.]

Section 3

4.3.1   New States may be admitted by the Congress into this Union; but no new State shall be formed or erected within the Jurisdiction of any other State; nor any State be formed by the Junction of two or more States, or Parts of States, without the Consent of the Legislatures of the States concerned as well as of the Congress.

4.3.2 The Congress shall have Power to dispose of and make all needful Rules and Regulations respecting the Territory or other Property belonging to the United States; and nothing in this Constitution shall be so construed as to Prejudice any Claims of the United States, or of any particular State.

Section 4

The United States shall guarantee to every State in this Union a Republican Form of Government, and shall protect each of them against Invasion; and on Application of the Legislature, or of the Executive (when the Legislature cannot be convened), against domestic Violence.

Article V

Section 1   The Congress, whenever two thirds of both Houses shall deem it necessary, shall propose Amendments to this Constitution, or, on the Application of the Legislatures of two thirds of the several States, shall call a Convention for proposing Amendments,

Section 2   which, in either Case, shall be valid to all Intents and Purposes, as Part of this Constitution, when ratified by the Legislatures of three fourths of the several States, or by Conventions in three fourths thereof, as the one or the other Mode of Ratification may be proposed by the Congress;

Section 3   Provided that no Amendment which may be made prior to the Year One thousand eight hundred and eight shall in any Manner affect the first and fourth Clauses in the Ninth Section of the first Article; and that no State, without its Consent, shall be deprived of its equal Suffrage in the Senate.

Article VI

Section 1 All Debts contracted and Engagements entered into, before the Adoption of this Constitution, shall be as valid against the United States under this Constitution, as under the Confederation.

Section 2 This Constitution, and the Laws of the United States which shall be made in Pursuance thereof; and all Treaties made, or which shall be made, under the Authority of the United States, shall be the supreme Law of the Land; and the Judges in every State shall be bound thereby, any Thing in the Constitution or Laws of any State to the Contrary notwithstanding.

Section 3 The Senators and Representatives before mentioned, and the Members of the several State Legislatures, and all executive and judicial Officers, both of the United States and of the several States, shall be bound by Oath or Affirmation, to support this Constitution; but no religious Test shall ever be required as a Qualification to any Office or public Trust under the United States.

Article VII

The Ratification of the Conventions of nine States, shall be sufficient for the Establishment of this Constitution between the States so ratifying the Same.

Done in Convention by the Unanimous Consent of the States present the Seventeenth Day of September in the Year of our Lord one thousand seven hundred and Eighty seven and of the Independence of the United States of America the Twelfth In witness whereof We have hereunto subscribed our Names,

Go. WASHINGTON — Presidt.
and deputy from Virginia

New Hampshire
JOHN LANGDON
NICHOLAS GILMAN
Massachusetts
NATHANIEL GORHAM
RUFUS KING
Connecticut
WM. SAML. JOHNSON
ROGER SHERMAN
New York
ALEXANDER HAMILTON
New Jersey
WIL: LIVINGSTON
DAVID BREARLEY.
WM. PATERSON.
JONA: DAYTON
Pennsylvania
B FRANKLIN
THOMAS MIFFLIN
ROBT MORRIS
GEO. CLYMER
THOS. FITZ SIMONS
JARED INGERSOLL
JAMES WILSON
GOUV MORRIS
Delaware
GEO: READ
GUNNING BEDFORD jun
JOHN DICKINSON
RICHARD BASSETT
JACO: BROOM
Maryland

JAMES MCHENRY
DAN OF ST THOS. JENIFER
DANL CARROLL
Virginia
JOHN BLAIR
JAMES MADISON jr
North Carolina
WM. BLOUNT
RICHD. DOBBS SPAIGHT
HU WILLIAMSON
South Carolina
J. RUTLEDGE
CHARLES COTESWORTH PINCKNEY
CHARLES PINCKNEY
PIERCE BUTLER
Georgia
WILLIAM FEW
ABR BALDWIN

In Convention Monday, September 17th, 1787.

Present

The States of

New Hampshire, Massachusetts, Connecticut, MR. Hamilton from New York, New Jersey, Pennsylvania, Delaware, Maryland, Virginia, North Carolina, South Carolina and Georgia.

Resolved,

That the preceding Constitution be laid before the United States in Congress assembled, and that it is the Opinion of this Convention, that it should afterwards be submitted to a Convention of Delegates, chosen in each State by the People thereof, under the Recommendation of its Legislature, for their Assent and Ratification; and that each Convention assenting to, and ratifying the Same, should give Notice thereof to the United States in Congress assembled.

Resolved, That it is the Opinion of this Convention, that as soon as the Conventions of nine States shall have ratified this Constitution, the United States in Congress assembled should fix a Day on which Electors should be appointed by the States which have ratified the same, and a Day on which the Electors should assemble to vote for the President, and the Time and Place for commencing Proceedings under this Constitution. That after such Publication the Electors should be appointed, and the Senators and Representatives elected:

That the Electors should meet on the Day fixed for the Election of the President, and should transmit their Votes certified, signed, sealed and directed, as the Constitution requires, to the Secretary of the United States in Congress assembled, that the Senators and Representatives should convene at the Time and Place assigned; that the Senators should appoint a President of the Senate, for the sole purpose of receiving, opening and counting the Votes for President; and, that after he shall be chosen, the Congress, together with the President, should, without Delay, proceed to execute this Constitution.

By the Unanimous Order of the Convention

Go. WASHINGTON — Presidt.
W. JACKSON Secretary

Amendments to the Constitution

On September 25, 1789, the First Congress of the United States proposed our Bill of Rights, the first 12 amendments to the Constitution. In Chapter 1 you learned that ten of the proposed twelve amendments were ratified by three-fourths of the state legislatures by 1791. Then in 1992, 203 years after the first states ratified it, Article 2 was ratified as the 27th Amendment. Article 1, requiring that no U.S. congressional district contain more than 50,000 persons, was ratified by 11 states. A coalition called Our First Right is working to gain ratification by 27 more states required to make it become the 28th Amendment.

The U.S. Bill of Rights

The Preamble to The Bill of Rights

Congress of the United States begun and held at the City of New-York, on Wednesday the fourth of March, one thousand seven hundred and eighty nine.

THE Conventions of a number of the States, having at the time of their adopting the Constitution, expressed a desire, in order to prevent misconstruction or abuse of its powers, that further declaratory and restrictive clauses should be added: And as extending the ground of public confidence in the Government, will best ensure the beneficent ends of its institution.

RESOLVED by the Senate and House of Representatives of the United States of America, in Congress assembled, two thirds of both Houses concurring, that the following Articles be proposed to the Legislatures of the several States, as amendments to the Constitution of the United States, all, or any of which Articles, when ratified by three fourths of the said Legislatures, to be valid to all intents and purposes, as part of the said Constitution; viz.

ARTICLES in addition to, and Amendment of the Constitution of the United States of America, proposed by Congress, and ratified by the Legislatures of the several States, pursuant to the fifth Article of the original Constitution.

Note: The following text is a transcription of the first ten amendments that were ratified, not including the original 'Article the First' and 'Article the Second'.

Amendment I

Congress shall make no law respecting an establishment of religion, or prohibiting the free exercise thereof; or abridging the freedom of speech, or of the press; or the right of the people peaceably to assemble, and to petition the Government for a redress of grievances.

Amendment II

A well regulated Militia, being necessary to the security of a free State, the right of the people to keep and bear Arms, shall not be infringed.

Amendment III

No Soldier shall, in time of peace be quartered in any house, without the consent of the Owner, nor in time of war, but in a manner to be prescribed by law.

Amendment IV

The right of the people to be secure in their persons, houses, papers, and effects, against unreasonable searches and seizures, shall not be violated, and no Warrants shall issue, but upon probable cause, supported by Oath or affirmation, and particularly describing the place to be searched, and the persons or things to be seized.

Amendment V

No person shall be held to answer for a capital, or otherwise infamous crime, unless on a presentment or indictment of a Grand Jury, except in cases arising in the land or naval forces, or in the Militia, when in actual service in time of War or public danger; nor shall any person be subject for the same offence to be twice put in jeopardy of life or limb; nor shall be compelled in any criminal case to be a witness against himself, nor be deprived of life, liberty, or property, without due process of law; nor shall private property be taken for public use, without just compensation.

Amendment VI

In all criminal prosecutions, the accused shall enjoy the right to a speedy and public trial, by an impartial jury of the State and district wherein the crime shall have been committed, which district shall have been previously ascertained by law, and to be informed of the nature and cause of the accusation; to be confronted with the witnesses against him; to have compulsory process for obtaining witnesses in his favor, and to have the Assistance of Counsel for his defence.

Amendment VII

In Suits at common law, where the value in controversy shall exceed twenty dollars, the right of trial by jury shall be preserved, and no fact tried by a jury, shall be otherwise re-examined in any Court of the United States, than according to the rules of the common law.

Amendment VIII

Excessive bail shall not be required, nor excessive fines imposed, nor cruel and unusual punishments inflicted.

Amendment IX

The enumeration in the Constitution, of certain rights, shall not be construed to deny or disparage others retained by the people.

Amendment X

The powers not delegated to the United States by the Constitution, nor prohibited by it to the States, are reserved to the States respectively, or to the people.

Amendment XI

Passed by Congress March 4, 1794. Ratified February 7, 1795.

Note: Article III, section 2, of the Constitution was modified by amendment 11.

The Judicial power of the United States shall not be construed to extend to any suit in law or equity, commenced or prosecuted against one of the United States by Citizens of another State, or by Citizens or Subjects of any Foreign State.

Amendment XII

Passed by Congress December 9, 1803. Ratified June 15, 1804.

Note: A portion of Article II, section 1 of the Constitution was superseded by the 12th amendment.

The Electors shall meet in their respective states and vote by ballot for President and Vice-President, one of whom, at least, shall not be an inhabitant of the same state with themselves; they shall name in their ballots the person voted for as President, and in distinct ballots the person voted for as Vice-President, and they shall make distinct lists of all persons voted for as President, and of all persons voted for as Vice-President, and of the number of votes for each, which lists they shall sign and certify, and transmit sealed to the seat of the government of the United States, directed to the President of the Senate; — the President of the Senate shall, in the presence of the Senate and House of Representatives, open all the certificates and the votes shall then be counted; — The person having the greatest number of votes for President, shall be the President, if such number be a majority of the whole number of Electors appointed; and if no person have such majority, then from the persons having the highest numbers not exceeding three on the list of those voted for as President, the House of Representatives shall choose immediately, by ballot, the President. But in choosing the President, the votes shall be taken by states, the representation from each state having one vote; a quorum for this purpose shall consist of a member or members from two-thirds of the states, and a majority of all the states shall be necessary to a choice. [And if the House of Representatives shall not choose a President whenever the right of choice shall devolve upon them, before the fourth day of March next following, then the Vice-President shall act as President, as in case of the death or other constitutional disability of the President. –]* The person having the greatest number of votes as Vice-President, shall be the Vice-President, if such number be a majority of the whole number of Electors appointed, and if no person have a majority, then from the two highest numbers on the list, the Senate shall choose the Vice-President; a quorum for the purpose shall consist of two-thirds of the whole number of Senators, and a majority of the whole number shall be necessary to a choice. But no person constitutionally ineligible to the office of President shall be eligible to that of Vice-President of the United States.

*Superseded by section 3 of the 20th amendment.

Amendment XIII

Passed by Congress January 31, 1865. Ratified December 6, 1865.

Note: A portion of Article IV, section 2, of the Constitution was superseded by the 13th amendment.

Section 1.

Neither slavery nor involuntary servitude, except as a punishment for crime whereof the party shall have been duly convicted, shall exist within the United States, or any place subject to their jurisdiction.

Section 2.

Congress shall have power to enforce this article by appropriate legislation.

Amendment XIV

Passed by Congress June 13, 1866. Ratified July 9, 1868.

Note*: Article I, section 2, of the Constitution was modified by section 2 of the 14th amendment.*

Section 1.

All persons born or naturalized in the United States, and subject to the jurisdiction thereof, are citizens of the United States and of the State wherein they reside. No State shall make or enforce any law which shall abridge the privileges or immunities of citizens of the United States; nor shall any State deprive any person of life, liberty, or property, without due process of law; nor deny to any person within its jurisdiction the equal protection of the laws.

Section 2.

Representatives shall be apportioned among the several States according to their respective numbers, counting the whole number of persons in each State, excluding Indians not taxed. But when the right to vote at any election for the choice of electors for President and Vice-President of the United States, Representatives in Congress, the Executive and Judicial officers of a State, or the members of the Legislature thereof, is denied to any of the male inhabitants of such State, being twenty-one years of age,* and citizens of the United States, or in any way abridged, except for participation in rebellion, or

124

other crime, the basis of representation therein shall be reduced in the proportion which the number of such male citizens shall bear to the whole number of male citizens twenty-one years of age in such State.

Section 3.

No person shall be a Senator or Representative in Congress, or elector of President and Vice-President, or hold any office, civil or military, under the United States, or under any State, who, having previously taken an oath, as a member of Congress, or as an officer of the United States, or as a member of any State legislature, or as an executive or judicial officer of any State, to support the Constitution of the United States, shall have engaged in insurrection or rebellion against the same, or given aid or comfort to the enemies thereof. But Congress may by a vote of two-thirds of each House, remove such disability.

Section 4.

The validity of the public debt of the United States, authorized by law, including debts incurred for payment of pensions and bounties for services in suppressing insurrection or rebellion, shall not be questioned. But neither the United States nor any State shall assume or pay any debt or obligation incurred in aid of insurrection or rebellion against the United States, or any claim for the loss or emancipation of any slave; but all such debts, obligations and claims shall be held illegal and void.

Section 5.

The Congress shall have the power to enforce, by appropriate legislation, the provisions of this article.

Changed by section 1 of the 26th amendment.

Amendment XV

Passed by Congress February 26, 1869. Ratified February 3, 1870.

Section 1.

The right of citizens of the United States to vote shall not be denied or abridged by the United States or by any State on account of race, color, or previous condition of servitude.

Section 2.

The Congress shall have the power to enforce this article by appropriate legislation.

Amendment XVI

Passed by Congress July 2, 1909. Ratified February 3, 1913.

Note: Article I, section 9, of the Constitution was modified by amendment 16, and that declaring "without regard to any census or enumeration" is akin to making a law that declares you do not have to obey the law.

The Congress shall have power to lay and collect taxes on incomes, from whatever source derived, without apportionment among the several States, and without regard to any census or enumeration.

Amendment XVII

Passed by Congress May 13, 1912. Ratified April 8, 1913.

Note: Article I, section 3, of the Constitution was modified by the 17th amendment.

The Senate of the United States shall be composed of two Senators from each State, elected by the people thereof, for six years; and each Senator shall have one vote. The electors in each State shall have the qualifications requisite for electors of the most numerous branch of the State legislatures.

When vacancies happen in the representation of any State in the Senate, the executive authority of such State shall issue writs of election to fill such vacancies: *Provided*, That the legislature of any State may empower the executive thereof to make temporary appointments until the people fill the vacancies by election as the legislature may direct.

This amendment shall not be so construed as to affect the election or term of any Senator chosen before it becomes valid as part of the Constitution.

Amendment XVIII

Passed by Congress December 18, 1917. Ratified January 16, 1919. Repealed by amendment 21.

Section 1.

After one year from the ratification of this article the manufacture, sale, or transportation of intoxicating liquors within, the importation thereof into, or the exportation thereof from the United States and all territory subject to the jurisdiction thereof for beverage purposes is hereby prohibited.

Section 2.

The Congress and the several States shall have concurrent power to enforce this article by appropriate legislation.

Section 3.

This article shall be inoperative unless it shall have been ratified as an amendment to the Constitution by the legislatures of the several States, as provided in the Constitution, within seven years from the date of the submission hereof to the States by the Congress.

Amendment XIX

Passed by Congress June 4, 1919. Ratified August 18, 1920.

The right of citizens of the United States to vote shall not be denied or abridged by the United States or by any State on account of sex.

Congress shall have power to enforce this article by appropriate legislation.

Amendment XX

Passed by Congress March 2, 1932. Ratified January 23, 1933.

Note: Article I, section 4, of the Constitution was modified by section 2 of this amendment. In addition, a portion of the 12th amendment was superseded by section 3.

Section 1.

The terms of the President and the Vice President shall end at noon on the 20th day of January, and the terms of Senators and Representatives at noon on the 3d day of January, of the years in which such terms would have ended if this article had not been ratified; and the terms of their successors shall then begin.

Section 2.

The Congress shall assemble at least once in every year, and such meeting shall begin at noon on the 3d day of January, unless they shall by law appoint a different day.

Section 3.

If, at the time fixed for the beginning of the term of the President, the President elect shall have died, the Vice President elect shall become President. If a President shall not have been chosen before the time fixed for the beginning of his term, or if the President elect shall have failed to qualify, then the Vice President elect shall act as President until a President shall have qualified; and the Congress may by law provide for the case wherein neither a President elect nor a Vice President elect shall have qualified, declaring who shall then act as President, or the manner in which one who is to act shall be selected, and such person shall act accordingly until a President or Vice President shall have qualified.

Section 4.

The Congress may by law provide for the case of the death of any of the persons from whom the House of Representatives may choose a President whenever the right of choice shall have devolved upon them, and for the case of the death of any of the persons from whom the Senate may choose a Vice President whenever the right of choice shall have devolved upon them.

Section 5.

Sections 1 and 2 shall take effect on the 15th day of October following the ratification of this article.

Section 6.

This article shall be inoperative unless it shall have been ratified as an amendment to the Constitution by the legislatures of three-fourths of the several States within seven years from the date of its submission.

Amendment XXI

Passed by Congress February 20, 1933. Ratified December 5, 1933.

Section 1.

The eighteenth article of amendment to the Constitution of the United States is hereby repealed.

Section 2.

The transportation or importation into any State, Territory, or possession of the United States for delivery or use therein of intoxicating liquors, in violation of the laws thereof, is hereby prohibited.

Section 3.

This article shall be inoperative unless it shall have been ratified as an amendment to the Constitution by conventions in the several States, as provided in the Constitution, within seven years from the date of the submission hereof to the States by the Congress.

Amendment XXII

Passed by Congress March 21, 1947. Ratified February 27, 1951.

Section 1.

No person shall be elected to the office of the President more than twice, and no person who has held the office of President, or acted as President, for more than two years of a term to which some other person was elected President shall be elected to the office of the President more than once. But this Article shall not apply to any person holding the office of President when this Article was proposed by the Congress, and shall not prevent any person who may be holding the office of President, or acting as President, during the term within which this Article becomes operative from holding the office of President or acting as President during the remainder of such term.

Section 2.

This article shall be inoperative unless it shall have been ratified as an amendment to the Constitution by the legislatures of three-fourths of the several States within seven years from the date of its submission to the States by the Congress.

Amendment XXIII

Passed by Congress June 16, 1960. Ratified March 29, 1961.

Section 1.

The District constituting the seat of Government of the United States shall appoint in such manner as the Congress may direct:

A number of electors of President and Vice President equal to the whole number of Senators and Representatives in Congress to which the District would be entitled if it were a State, but in no event more than the least populous State; they shall be in addition to those appointed by the States, but they shall be considered, for the purposes of the election of President and Vice President, to be electors appointed by a State; and they shall meet in the District and perform such duties as provided by the twelfth article of amendment.

Section 2.

The Congress shall have power to enforce this article by appropriate legislation.

Amendment XXIV

Passed by Congress August 27, 1962. Ratified January 23, 1964.

Section 1.

The right of citizens of the United States to vote in any primary or other election for President or Vice President, for electors for President or Vice President, or for Senator or Representative in Congress, shall not be denied or abridged by the United States or any State by reason of failure to pay any poll tax or other tax.

Section 2.

The Congress shall have power to enforce this article by appropriate legislation.

Amendment XXV

Passed by Congress July 6, 1965. Ratified February 10, 1967.

Note: Article II, section 1, of the Constitution was affected by the 25th amendment.

Section 1.

In case of the removal of the President from office or of his death or resignation, the Vice President shall become President.

Section 2.

Whenever there is a vacancy in the office of the Vice President, the President shall nominate a Vice President who shall take office upon confirmation by a majority vote of both Houses of Congress.

Section 3.

Whenever the President transmits to the President pro tempore of the Senate and the Speaker of the House of Representatives his written declaration that he is unable to discharge the powers and duties of his office, and until he transmits to them a written declaration to the contrary, such powers and duties shall be discharged by the Vice President as Acting President.

Section 4.

Whenever the Vice President and a majority of either the principal officers of the executive departments or of such other body as Congress may by law provide, transmit to the President pro tempore of the Senate and the Speaker of the House of Representatives their written declaration that the President is unable to discharge the powers and duties of his office, the Vice President shall immediately assume the powers and duties of the office as Acting President.

Thereafter, when the President transmits to the President pro tempore of the Senate and the Speaker of the House of Representatives his written declaration that no inability exists, he shall resume the powers and duties of his office unless the

Vice President and a majority of either the principal officers of the executive department or of such other body as Congress may by law provide, transmit within four days to the President pro tempore of the Senate and the Speaker of the House of Representatives their written declaration that the President is unable to discharge the powers and duties of his office. Thereupon Congress shall decide the issue, assembling within forty-eight hours for that purpose if not in session. If the Congress, within twenty-one days after receipt of the latter written declaration, or, if Congress is not in session, within twenty-one days after Congress is required to assemble, determines by two-thirds vote of both Houses that the President is unable to discharge the powers and duties of his office, the Vice President shall continue to discharge the same as Acting President; otherwise, the President shall resume the powers and duties of his office.

Amendment XXVI

Passed by Congress March 23, 1971. Ratified July 1, 1971.

Amendment 14, section 2 was modified by this section 1.

Section 1.

The right of citizens of the United States, who are eighteen years of age or older, to vote shall not be denied or abridged by the United States or by any State on account of age.

Section 2.

The Congress shall have power to enforce this article by appropriate legislation.

Amendment XXVII

Originally proposed Sept. 25, 1789. Ratified May 7, 1992.

No law, varying the compensation for the services of the Senators and Representatives, shall take effect, until an election of Representatives shall have intervened.

About the Author

David M. Zuniga is a graduate of the University of Texas (BS, Architectural Engineering); for 28 years a professional engineer designing schools, churches, industrial and commercial buildings, David has been a cattleman, custom homebuilder, commercial contractor, residential and industrial land developer, book editor, SCUBA instructor, missionary pilot, and land surveyor. He founded four classical Christian K-12 schools in three states, including Latin, Logic, Rhetoric, and the Great Books.

Shocked at our own government attacking us on 9/11, in 2006 he began 14 months in monastic seclusion, prayer and study of 110 books, after which he drafted the *AmericaAgain! Declaration.* He refined the document with the help of many Americans including radio host Mike Church and constitutional scholar and author Edwin Vieira Jr.

Establishing AmericaAgain! Trust with his brother in 2009, David wrote his first book *This Bloodless Liberty* in 2010 to convey his vision and in 2015, his book *Fear The People* began to flesh out the details. He is now writing a 7-volume library to give every TACTICAL CIVICS™ chapter a full, step-by-step guide to this new way of life: the end of politics and the beginning of true popular sovereignty for the first time in history.

David has been a guest on Infowars Nightly News and on radio shows across America. His articles have appeared on many blogs, forums and alternative media.

David and his wife of 41 years have two children and six grandchildren. They live in the Hill Country of Texas where they serve No king but King Jesus.

Made in the USA
Las Vegas, NV
29 June 2021